D0365734

To Bob & Suzanne

Biblical, P.C.,
and with that typeface
I like - couldn't resist.

Love, Lisa

Also by Edward P. Moser

*The Politically Correct Guide to American History*

# The Politically Correct Guide to

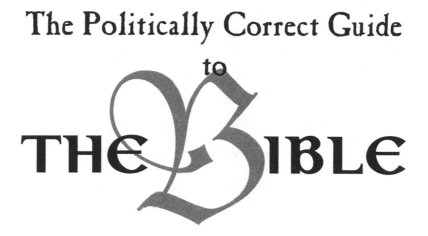

THE BIBLE

## EDWARD P. MOSER

CROWN PUBLISHERS, INC.
NEW YORK

Copyright © 1997 by Edward P. Moser

All rights reserved. No part of this book may be reproduced or trans-
mitted in any form or by any means, electronic or mechanical, including photocopying, recording, or by any information storage and
retrieval system, without permission in writing from the publisher.

Published by Crown Publishers, Inc., 201 East 50th Street, New York,
New York 10022. Member of the Crown Publishing Group.

Random House, Inc. New York, Toronto, London, Sydney, Auckland

http://www.randomhouse.com/

CROWN and colophon are trademarks of Crown Publishers, Inc.

Printed in the United States of America

Library of Congress Cataloging-in-Publication Data
Moser, Edward P.
    The politically correct guide to the Bible / Edward P. Moser.
        p.   cm.
    Includes index.
    1. Bible—Humor.   2. Political correctness—Humor.   3. American
wit and humor.   I. Title.
    PN6231.B45M67   1997
    220'.02'07—dc21                         96-51708
                                              CIP

ISBN 0-517-70789-6

10   9   8   7   6   5   4   3   2   1

First Edition

To Cara, Donna, Erica, and Matt

# ✢ Contents ✢

# ❧ Acknowledgments ❧

Thanks again to J & R for the time, and to Michael & Linda for the same. Also to J & M for their dogged attendance at auctorial events, and Trammel, Mike P., and the mailing list for the sounding boards.

Much thanks to the Daniel Bial Agency for placing this book, and to Dan's keen criticism and suggestions.

And once again to Carol Taylor and the Crown team, for their editorial judgment, production skills, and marketing flair. To Philip Bliss for the arresting cover art. And Jim & Co. for the penultimate read. A special word of gratitude for Elke and Shanna's promotional blitz.

Much thanks for the inspiration: Henry Beard, Warren Brookes, Bill Cosby ("Noah"), George Carlin, *Duck Soup*, J. P. Dunleavy, William C. Fields, William Gaines, Larry Gelbart, Howard Hawks, Tony Hendra, Paul Johnson, *Dr. Strangelove*, Lucian (especially "A True Story"), Michael O'Donoghue, Rabelais, Steven Wright, Zucker-Zucker-Abraham, and George Orwell.

All chapters courtesy of Laputa Isle Projections.

Let us go down,

and there confound their language,

that they may not understand

one another's speech. . . .

Therefore is the name of it

called Babel.

GENESIS 11:7–9

Sensitive readers are forewarned they may be disturbed by some of the accounts and descriptions contained herein. Each book purchaser, therefore, is asked to sign the following prereading agreement, which absolves the author of legal liability for mental or physical disabilities resulting from examination of the text:

*I hereby certify that the writer, or the companies supplying him with pen and ink to construct this document, shall not be held responsible for any psychological trauma, medical conditions, or toxic chemicals acquired from turning the pages of* The Politically Correct Guide to the Bible.

Signed,

_____

The Politically Correct Guide

to

THE IBLE

# In the Beginning

In the beginning—assuming there was a beginning, as opposed to an endless cycle—in the beginning, God—assuming he, she, or it exists— in the beginning, God created the heaven and the earth. And God said, "Let there be light," and noticed the light, for God was not visually disadvantaged. And God saw the light was good, making an unprovable value judgment. And * said, "Let there be a firmament, dividing the waters above it from the waters below," and God

---

*God. Atheists offended by the presumption of a divine being may substitute an asterisk for the term "God."

called the firmament Heaven. No slight was intended to Hell, which was created later.

And God said, to no one in particular, "Let the dry land appear. Let the earth bring forth grass, and herb-bearing seed." And God experienced short-term memory loss and a severe case of the munchies, although the Supreme Being didn't inhale.

And God made two great lights in the sky; the more stature-endowed light to rule the day, and the less stature-enhanced to rule the night. And both the sun and the moon it lit were solar-powered.

And God said, "Let the waters and the earth bring forth every living creature." For God was not a creationist, but an ardent believer in the theory of evolution.

And god* made the animal companion of the earth after his kind, and made the cattle after her kind, and every thing that creepeth upon the earth after their kind. And God said, "To every animal companion, cattle, and creeping thing, I have given tree-yielding seed, and it shall be as meat." For all creatures are meant to be vegetarians.

And on the seventh day of creation, God took a mental health day. Thus the heavens and earth and sea and all their hosts and hostesses were finished in only six days. This may indicate God was not, as is commonly thought, an elderly Jewish man, but a Methodist, for God clearly had a Protestant work ethic.

And thus it began.

*Pagan believers objecting to the large letter G in God may spell the word with a small g.

# ve and Adam's Patriarchal Oppressor

And lo, it was a sexist thing to make a man before a womyn. But God fancied making man after his own image. Perhaps he wanted company, having been pretty much on his own for five billion years. The deity breathed into Adam's nostrils the breath of life, pushed hard upon his chest, applied the electric-shock paddles of life, and man became a living being. God placed his creation in a garden lush with fruit, which raised moral dilemmas about eating fruit. For mangoes and figs have feelings too, as evidenced by their strong response to stimuli like sunlight and recorded music.

The deity told Adam, "Behold, I have given you herb-bearing seed, and its grass is upon the face of all the earth," and Adam experienced temporary memory loss, and fashioned the Middle East's first hookah.

God had Adam name all the animals, without first asking their permission. The critters were not asked to name Adam and God in return. Forced to devise terms for tens of thousands of species, Adam cleverly started with the word aardvark; the two initial As ensured he wouldn't run out of letters. By the time he got to yak and zebra, however, Adam was ready for the world's first vacation!

Censorship began as God approved most of Adam's nominations but vetoed offensive terms like derriere (ass).

The Lord said, "It isn't left* that the man should be alone. Sure, a bachelor like Adam may think he's living in paradise. He doesn't have to commit to any relationship. He can always get out of doing the yard work (an important perk, given the extent of his verdant garden). But a single guy's more likely to be stressed-out, depressed, or infirm, and to suffer from a statistically lower life span."

So the Patriarchal Oppressor made another being, without asking her permission either. In fashioning Eve from Adam's rib, the deity did not collect the required medical papers for approval of the bone transplant. The first man was, however, given an Adam's apple as nonmonetary compensation. The Lord caused a deep sleep to fall upon Adam, despite the risk of being sued over an allergic reaction to the strong anesthesia. God said, "She shall be her husband's help

---

*Right. Use of the term "right" reinforces pervasive bias against left-handed people.

mate," before amending that to, "She shall be a full partner in a coequal relationship."

The male-femail coupling was not meant to slur those of alternative gender preference. The deity could just as easily have created two gals or two guys. The sexes chosen were hardly of consequence, for one's gender is ever in a state of flux, subject to mood, age, culture, and social pressures.

God brought Eve to the man, and the man made the world's first sexist remark: "Hey, God, if you can make more babes, I got plenty of ribs." Adam then made the world's second sexist remark: "She shall be called Womyn, because she was taken out of Myn."

And the man and womyn were naked, and unabashedly unashamed. For they had great bods, due to their fruity, high-fiber diet. Sprung into creation fully formed, they were spared the erosive effects of gravity and time.

Eve in particular gloried in the clothing-optional lifestyle. No chest shackle embodying an all-consuming male oppression interned her liberated physique, displayed as naturally as a topless bather on a Mediterranean beach. With risk of visual harassment from only one man on earth, Eve confidently roamed the garden stripped to the ankles. The earth mother shunned the blush and eyeliner ripped from sentient sea beings to trap womynfolk in unrealistic expectations of timeless beauty.

The Patriarchal Oppressor swiftly moved to replace Eve's freedom with the prison of raising a family, saying, "Be fruitful and multiply." Adam replied, "How can we multiply when the indigenous peoples of the Middle East haven't invented Arabic numbers yet?"

Eve answered, "I think he means procreate. But we should limit ourselves to 2.3 children, or whatever the replacement rate is for zero population growth." Eve wished, if multiply she must, to delay childbearing until the invention of herding and agriculture allowed her to establish a career. The first feminist would have preferred to procreate by herself—she sensed an all-womyn world would have dramatically lowered crime and school-dropout rates—but artificial insemination wasn't yet a viable option.

God stated, "Let womyn and myn have dominion over all the earth, and subdue it, and rule over the fish, fowl, and cattle companions, and every creeping thing." Despite the obvious injustice to nonhumans of this naked land grab, the humans were tempted by the offer of power. Eve answered, "What if we accept, but you get to keep the creeping things?"

But the Land Lord said it was an all-or-nothing deal. God then reneged on his territorial grant, forbidding the couple to eat from the Tree of the Knowledge of Societally Sanctioned and Ethically Challenged Behavior.*

In the common-law marriage that followed, Eve and Adam noticed that, although any real differences between the sexes are of course minuscule, their behavior did occasionally diverge. Adam left banana peels and orange rinds all over the garden floor, which Eve preferred to keep spotless. Although her novel means of birth had been truly unforgettable, Adam usually forgot Eve's birthday. Although Eden's living conditions were ideal, Eve prodded Adam into building a tree house and, after its construction, to make constant domestic improvements. Despite these minor disagreements, Eve and Adam lived well-adjusted lives with high levels of self-esteem, when suddenly their world turned upside down.

In all creation, the serpentine companion was the most cerebrally advantaged, with the possible exception of dolphins, chimpanzees, and porcine companions, which, contrary to speciestic bias, are quite intelligent and not that

---

*Tree of the Knowledge of Good and Evil. "Good" and "evil" are unprovable value judgments.

sloppy. The serpent was a founding member of a misunderstood satanic cult unjustly expelled from a paradise of its own without trial or benefit of attorney. Denied a safety net to ease a precipitous plunge into Hell and asbestos clothing to protect against the fires of its new home, the snake bore a justifiable grudge against the deity.

*Although the asbestos, as a carcinogenic material, might have caused even more harm,* it thought. *Whenever my skin was scorched I could just slough it off.* After a six-thousand-year sentence, with no time off for acceptable behavior, the creature was finally up before the parole board, and had been awarded a weekend furlough on earth.

The serpentine companion told Eve, "Empower thyself, and taste of the tree's fruit. Reach your full human potential by rejecting God's crass obsession with property lefts. You and Adam have lived here long enough to insist on squatters' lefts, and demand full and equal access to every place in the garden. As for the tree, there's no Alar on its apples.

"I assure thee, ye shall surely not die, for if the Land Lord declined capital punishment for a repeat offender like me, he'll surely spare the life of his favorite creations. Besides, this 'knowledge of good and evil' stuff poses a false moral dichotomy. Allegedly wrongful behavior only reflects varying cultural perspectives."

The serpent also offered the lusty but naive first couple tips on provocative procreative procedures.

Despite reservations about creeping things, Eve took the serpent's advice. *It's only a harmless garden snake,* she figured. Eve partook of the tree, and shared her fruit with her Significant Other. Contrary to general belief, she offered not an apple, but passion fruit. After Adam partook, Eve felt vague misgivings, but couldn't share her thoughts because Adam, like every man since, had fallen immediately asleep.

When they awoke the next dawn, Eve felt awkward, while

Adam felt an overpowering desire to go to his own tree house. Both felt an irrational sense of damaged self-esteem, or shame, and remorse over trampling on some arbitrarily chosen moral principle.

Suddenly uneasy about their nakedness, they found they could hide it in two ways. By sewing together fig leaves they made aprons, which let Adam demonstrate myn are as much at home in the kitchen as womyn. Further, by carefully choosing where they stood, they put strategically placed foliage between themselves and any outside observers.

One afternoon Eve and Adam heard the Land Lord's voice in the garden. (God relieved the stress of running the universe by going slumming on earth in human form.) While power-walking through the expropriated property, the deity sang: "He's got the whole world, in his hands/He's got the whole world, in his hands/He's got the whole world in his hands."

As God passed the Tree of the Knowledge of Societally Sanctioned and Ethically Challenged Behavior, his earth-shattering voice boomed: "Who's been eating from my tree?!" Eve and Adam hid among the shrubs, an understandable act given their battered self-esteem, but futile given the Land Lord's special powers. The serpent stayed where it was, and stuck a slimy, bifurcated tongue out at its former boss.

Resistance was futile, so Adam confessed. "I'm so embarrassed," he cried, "over spending the night with Eve."

"Who told you you're supposed to feel shame about that?!" the Prime Patriarch thundered. He turned to Eve. "I perceive you've eaten of the fruit—what's your excuse?"

"The serpent companion beguiled me."

"What's your excuse?" the snake was asked.

"The Devil made me do it."

The Patriarchal Oppressor rebuked Eve: "At least you could have gotten married first!" Then he took Adam aside, slapped him playfully on the shoulders, and winked. "Boys will be boys!"

Adam informed God he had another excuse. "I was sexually harassed, Lord. Eve made unwanted advances. She abused her position of power and authority, as the only other person on the planet, to coerce me into undesirable acts." Adam tried persuading God that female-on-male harassment was a growing trend, and in fact accounted for one hundred percent of the reported cases in Eden. But the Patriarchal Oppressor stereotypically thought that any man was physically strong and financially secure enough to fend off unsolicited urgings from the opposite sex.

The serpent, playing Devil's advocate, argued that Eve and Adam weren't responsible for their actions. "Created as fully formed adults," it snickered, "they were denied the innocence of childhood. As the first people, they had no siblings or parents to serve as nurturing role models. They've spent a frustrating life in a bootless search for their nonexistent inner child."

As thunder roared like an angry gavel, God canceled the snake's weekend furlough, denied its parole, and reassigned it a lifetime sentence in Hell. After filing an appeal, the serpent companion won a more lenient sentence, whereby it would forever crawl on its belly and eat dust.

The Land Lord also punished the humans. Under a cruel workfare plan, Eve and Adam were evicted without notice and made to sweat for a living, placed at the untender mercies of free-market forces. "Let them pull themselves up by their sandal straps!" God roared. The Land Lord enforced the expulsion by surrounding the gates of Eden with cherubs. Because no one was intimidated by the dimple-cheeked, angelic infants, he armed them with flaming swords. The Middle East has staggered since from a spiraling arms race.

God told Eve, "In sorrow shalt thou bring forth children," and Eve replied, "What's this bringing-forth business? Adam's got plenty of ribs left. I thought you just stood by the fruit tree and waited for your offspring to drop off fully formed." When informed of the harsh facts of life, Eve commented, "How about easing the pain with comprehensive day care?"

The Lord continued, "Thy husband shall rule over thee," and winked, and Eve winked back, for they knew that a Jewish wife runs the family. And God whispered to Eve, "Adam shall hearken unto the voice of his domestic partner."

God told Adam, "Cursed is the ground for thy sake; thorns and thistles shall it bring forth," and Adam replied, "Some revelation—what else should one expect from farming in an arid region?" Adam asked when he could apply for food stamps, but when met with stony silence began planning to till the soil.

Refusing to enslave oxen companions with a yoke, Adam put himself in the harness, then reasoned he could benefit the oxen with daily meals and protection from their natural enemies, and the yoke was on them. Still overburdened, he took out ads for farm help but for some reason received no reply. He steeply discounted the price of his produce but received no offers. Then he realized demand creates its own supply, and he and Eve begat Cain and Abel and a slew of other progeny, and food prices soared.

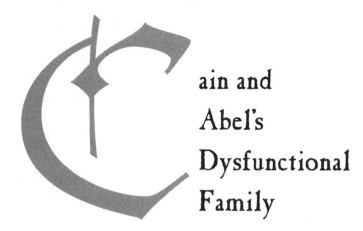

# Cain and Abel's Dysfunctional Family

Cain was a peaceful macrobiotic farmer, Abel a jailer of innocent sheep. Each had sexist attitudes. Both Cain and Abel were empty nesters, not because they disliked preadults,* or had alternate gender preferences, but because there weren't any daughters yet. In an attempt to bribe God into providing them with women, both offered a sacrifice. To supply a sacri-

---

*Children. The derisive terms "children" and "teenagers" imply that preadults should be denied the same prerogatives, such as marriage and military service, enjoyed by the more chronologically gifted.

ficial lamb, Abel murdered the defenseless firstborn sheep of his animal inmates, and the high-cholesterol fat thereof. Cain offered a platter of delectable, low-calorie fruit.

"Dear Lord," prayed the siblings, "blonds would be nice, but we're not choosy."

But the Lord rejected their entreaty, and Cain projected his disappointment onto Abel. Cain was very wroth, and his countenance fell—he later pleaded temporary insanity. While in the fields with Abel he rose up, that is, he raised Cain, and slew his sibling. Cain was a person with difficult-to-meet needs.

When God took his morning jog through the neighborhood, he spied Cain fleeing on a cart pulled by a white bronco. God snapped his fingers, and instantly the white bronco was trailed by dozens of chariots driven by cherubim with blazing swords. Cain was pulled over to the side of a path.

"License and identification, please," asked the chief cherub, who checked the ID against Hell's list of Most Wanted. The angel noted the driver's license number—000000000000000000000003—and the license checked out.

God asked Cain, "Where's Abel?" and Cain misstated the facts: "I know not—am I my sibling's keeper?" Then Cain made an incriminating remark. After apologizing for enslaving an animal companion, he noted that horses are "great for making getaways." He later claimed he meant "vacation getaway," not an escape from a crime. The fact that his saddlebag was filled with food and precious personal items could have borne out either interpretation.

The Higher Authority and his ethereal posse compiled a mountain of evidence implicating Cain. They found his horse cart set at a crazy angle to his curb, as if he'd parked it in a distracted rush. A bloody sickle was discovered outside his hut. Strands of Cain's hair and fibers from his tunic were found on Abel's remains. God mumbled something about deoxyribonucleic acid that went clear over the uneducated farmer's head.

The evidence was tarnished somewhat when a cherub collecting evidence was overheard making prejudicial remarks against humans. "I'm revolted by those flesh-and-blood mortals," the angel said. "They cause most of the trouble in what used to be a paradise on earth. Maybe they were made in God's image, but they weren't made in mine." Cain later accused the cherub of planting the bloody sickle.

But Cain's conflicting statements undermined his case. "It's a fact I tried to flee," he told the arresting angel, "but the sudden death of Abel unnerved me. From the start, everyone's acted like I was the only suspect, as if I was one of the only men on earth."

Later he retracted his alibi about a vacation getaway. "I left to tell Eve and Adam about the tragedy—yes, that's it. I was afraid a stranger might break the news to them first."

God noted his fear was unfounded as Cain was indeed, apart from Eve and Adam, the only other person on earth.

The suspect replied, "Actually, Adam did it—or Eve. I was rushing to their home to warn whichever one was innocent that she or he was in grave danger. Believe me, Lord, I was trying to find the real murderer."

Cain admitted to having harbored negative feelings toward the dearly departed: "As the first, more seasoned male sibling, Abel was always bossing me around. He used to beat me up, and tell on me to Adam: I suffered from post-traumatic stress syndrome. When I was very young he'd dress me up in Eve's clothing—not that there's anything wrong with dressing up in women's clothing. He always won the playground sports we played: Having invented the games, he knew all the rules— I didn't stand a chance!"

God asked Cain where he was at the time of the smiting.

"In the field with Abel—no, at my home. My place. I was gathering fruit, squeezing oranges, making juice—yes, it was O.J."

God asked if he had done anything else that day.

"I stood in my front yard practicing my sickle swing. Wait, that sounds sinister—it can't be true. In fact, I couldn't have practiced my sickle stroke because I have arthritis—the damp and chill, you know, from no central heating. Besides, I was lugging in very heavy packages, so I didn't have time to practice."

"How did you get that gash on your finger?"

"I cut my finger while plucking a harp."

"But your descendant Jubal won't invent musical instruments for six more generations."

"I was practicing my sickle swing."

Abel's defense was shaky, and it wasn't helped when the forked-tongue serpent of Eden offered to speak as a character witness in his defense. "We should move this investigation," suggested the snake companion, "to a more favorable venue, such as Hell." But the Lord disdained the serpent, who thought Creation a conspiracy of God to control the Universe, and rejected its advice.

Sensing the judgment of a wrathful God would go against him, Cain allowed how he might have done the deed. "But if I did," he said, "I had plenty of excuses.

"I grew up in the world's first dysfunctional family," he explained. "Pop was never home—forced to invent agriculture out of whole cloth, he labored day and night by the sweat of his brow. Mom, sadly for her, was *always* home, tending me and Abel. She was tormented her gender got stuck with the task of childbearing.

"When we were grown, Eve insisted on getting a part-time job picking apples. Adam's fragile ego was already bruised from rejection by God himself; it dissolved at his inability to fully provide for his family.

"At age four hundred, Adam had a midlife crisis. Women age less well than men, and once Eve entered her late three hundreds, Adam no longer found her attractive. Yes, it was selfish of him, after all those centuries of sharing Creation with Eve. Still, Adam would have had an affair if another woman had been available, but of course there wasn't, which just added to his frustration.

"I absorbed my parents' pent-up rage, Lord. Their anger simmered deep inside me for years, before exploding in a spontaneous act of violence against Abel. Therefore I really had nothing to do with his death. Everybody makes mistakes—I just want to get on with my life."

God rejected Cain's heartfelt rationales and held him, as he had Cain's parents, liable for his actions. God cursed the ground Cain tilled, breaking his own commandment against cursing. In a perhaps cruel and certainly unusual punishment, the Lord stamped on the forehead of the accursed the telltale Mark of Cain. The disfigurement trampled Cain's civil liberties, as the scar would remain long after any term of punishment. Worse, his medical plan didn't cover corrective surgery. Cain was ordered to undergo therapeutic counseling and perform three hundred hours of community service.

Unable to wring a living from the accursed soil, Cain took advantage of the burgeoning population from his parents' many later offspring. He went on a speaking tour and raked in huge fees while declaiming his innocence in Abel's slaying. Regarding his parents' late-blooming fertility, Cain figured, *It must be the rhinoceros horn powder that Adam consumes. He's six hundred years young and as frisky as ever.*

Like his dad, Cain exploited the lengthy life spans of biblical times. On his 150th birthday, after the statute of limitations ran out, Cain admitted to offing Abel. In the speaking

having made any persons in the first place. She said, "I will diss them all clear out of Creation."

Only Noah found grace in the eyes of the Lady. Noah never left the tap water dripping at the oasis. He separated out his trash before disposing of it. Humyn persons would nod approvingly of him and say, "Noah is a lefteous man."

One day, the Lady spoke to Noah while he was hiking along a desert nature trail in quiet communion with a host of deadly scorpions, poisonous spiders, venomous serpents, and other benign citizens of that fragile ecosystem.

"Because of humynkind's destructive ways," intoned the Lady, "the ozone layer has been depleted. Solar radiation is pouring in to melt the world's snow and ice. Rising temperatures shall engender relentless rainstorms, and bring forth a Great Flood. Every animal habitat will disappear."

"But, Lady," responded Noah, "didn't we just have the coolest summer on record? And the coldest winter?"

Ignoring the irreverent rejoinder, she ordered Noah to build a wooden ark 160 meters* in length. Goddess stressed she wanted a ship, not a Biosphere. In response, Noah asked for an advance and a binding contractual agreement. "If I'm to take off time from work," he noted, "I'll need a guarantee of compensation."

The Lady replied, "Take yourself and your sons Shem, Japaneseheth (Japheth), Processed-Pig-Carcass (Ham), and their Significant Others into the ark. I will establish with you a covenant."

"What's a covenant?" replied Noah, who apparently hadn't seen *Raiders of the Lost Ark*. But Goddess abruptly ended the labor negotiations.

---

*300 cubits. This document follows the metric system of weights and measures, as opposed to English and Hebraic systems based on the body parts—for example, "feet"—of deceased monarchical and patriarchal oppressors.

Alarmed by the warming warning, Noah started a grass-roots lobbying campaign to place every plant and animal on an Endangered Species List, but rain clouds were gathering faster than he could collect signatures for his petition. So he focused on building the ark.

When Noah placed his shipyard on a mountainside, cynics had thought him emotionally challenged for building a boat far from the water. But the high-altitude mountainside stayed temperate even as the rest of the world sweltered from the greenhouse effect.

It was fortunate Noah was only six hundred years young, with expectations of reaching one thousand, for construction of the ark was expensive and slow. Noah unionized his shipyard workers, and ordered them to demand higher wages from him. An early proponent of animal lefts, he forbade the use of horses and donkeys to haul heavy loads. Laborers falling off Jacob's ladder sued for workmen's comp. By law, Noah had to make the ark out of recycled wood products, so he scoured the barren Middle East for discarded palm logs and fallen eucalyptus trees.

Trouble also beset the other main construction project of the era, a tower at Babel that reached up toward heaven. Goddess realized such a large public works project constituted "trickle-up" economics, which spurred social equity with high-paying jobs. But the hard-hatted laborers were disturbingly genderist; they loudly complimented nubile womyn who happened by the building site at lunch hour.

A wrathful Lady said, "I will confound the workers' language, that they may not understand their own insensitive remarks." And lo, each worker spake different tongues, and construction ground to a halt. Then bilingual education programs were mandated, especially in Ebonics, and communication was restored. Diversity training sessions ended the verbal harassment. Its consciousness raised, the work force turned the tower into high-rise public housing.

When the ark was finally built, Noah islamic-judeo-christened it by smashing a bottle of nonalcoholic grape beverage against the hull. He then sent out a team of naturalists to collect two members of every species. However, because the naturalists did not discriminate on the basis of gender, the goal of collecting a male and female from each species was not met. This may explain puzzling gaps in the fossil record unearthed by modern scientists.

Because of the craft's titanic size, Noah was able to practice progressive methods of animal wifery. Instead of being caged, animal residents freely roamed open spaces simulating their natural habitats. Luckily, the incessant rains helped clear the decks of the creatures' prodigious waste matter production. Despite the happiness of the uncaged creatures, their human companions grew morose from a weeks-long absence of sunlight. The only crew members who enjoyed the voyage were the weatherpersons, who always revel in the attention that natural disasters bring them.

Noah forbade persons to call the ark a "zoo," a word with negative connotations concerning imprisonment of nonhumyn animals and denial of their universal right to due process (not to mention the trampled-on right of plants to *dew process*). He also rejected the term "wildlife center" for his ark because "wild" implied the nonhumyn residents were somehow savage or otherwise inferior. Legal documents referred to the ship as a biological diversity preservation center.

The ship's leader, who had something of a reactionary streak, was a firm believer in Goddess. However, Noah was careful—lest he be stoned for insensitivity—to encourage his crew's religious diversity. Beside a small temple to the Lady, a shrine was built for worshippers of Beelzebub.

As foretold, the heat and humidity from the planetary warming generated record rains that lasted eight five-day extended weather forecasts, or forty days and forty nights, and triggered widespread flooding. Before they were drowned, authorities declared most low-lying districts disaster areas and offered to pay ninety percent of the damage. Before they were drowned, critics complained the compensation would only encourage residence in flood-prone areas.

Surging seas climbed the mountain holding the ark and swept the boat up in a swirling current. Human and nonhuman residents panicked when the ship started to leak. The ark was saved when Noah lightened its load by releasing the vast collection of marine species. Expelling the whales alone lowered the ship's water line by several centimeters.

Eventually the rains stopped, and the waves receded. The ark came to rest atop Mount Ararat* in the modern country of Flightless Bird.† A rainbow representing a grand coalition of all disenfranchised peoples shimmered through scoured, pollution-free skies to smile on Noah and his biological preservation project.

Noah wanted to release a dove to see if the land was dry enough for the passengers to disembark. But when animal lefts activists opposed the experiment, Noah begged off. Conservatives among the crew wanted to release a hawk, but were outvoted. When he went to send a dove a second time, civil lefts activists protested the symbolism of sending a melanin-impoverished bird first. So Noah agreed to release a bird of color, a coal-black raven, before unleashing the dove. Spotted owls, an endangered species of mixed black-and-white ancestry, were too precious to risk on the perilous mission.

After the dove returned with the branch of an olive, whose

---

*No relation to Arafat, the whiskered champion of progressive armed struggle (terrorism) of a later era, who eventually betrayed his revolution by seeking peace, after a fashion, with the descendants of the Israelites.

† Turkey. The term "turkey," which slurs competency-challenged persons, and which is a constant reminder of the annual "Thanksgiving" slaughter of voiceless, defenseless (and flightless) poultry victims, should be avoided.

oil is renowned for its low cholesterol, the nonhumans left the ark. They reclaimed their former ecological niches cheered by new bans on hunting, zoos, and pet ownership. Because the ark was too far from the ocean for further use in seafaring, the crew dragged it over to a lumber recycling center. Noah urged everyone to shun open-air burning of sacrificial lambs and to engage in strict family planning marked by safe-sex practices like onanism.

# be, Sarah, and Cruelty to Animal Companions

Abe* was a fiscally endowed tent dweller who inherited a fortune in enslaved camels, goats, and sheep. His sheep community was particularly oppressed. Twice yearly, lambs were shorn of their very hair and left to nakedly endure the desert's nocturnal chill. Daily they had to sip from a dirty, disease-ridden trough of communal water. Forced into impersonal flocks by the savage blow of shepherds'

---

*Abraham. It is current common practice to refer even to venerable figures such as prophets and presidents in an informal, first-name basis.

staffs, they were denied the droughts, starvation, and mountain lion attacks of their natural habitat. An entire vocabulary of verbal slurs sprung up, deriding their character and courage with terms like "sheepish," "bleating like a lamb," "has the woollies."

Guard dogs co-opted by the human power structure viciously barked and nipped sheep into line. The canines themselves were collared with dog tags that reduced their personality and non-humanity to mere numbers. Generations of subservience and repressed anger among the hounds spawned weird behavioral disorders. Dogs were plagued by excessive salivation, sweaty paws, and an obsession for sticks tossed into ponds.

One day, while Abe was pondering ways to alleviate the plight of his animal companions, he heard the words of the Lord.

"Lift up thine eyes, Abe, and all the Land of Canaan which thou see is thine for everlasting possession." But Abe asked, "Lord, isn't such encroachment an act of imperialism? Is it fair to the native peoples of the region? Shouldn't they be consulted, along with the indigenous nonhuman animals?"

The Lord spake, "Abe, I shall make thy life partner Sarah the mother of many nations. I will multiply her eggs and thy seed to outnumber the stars and starlets of the heavens, and the sands upon the shore." Abe responsibly replied, "Lord, in the interest of sustainable growth, how about making our progeny as numerous as the humps on a camel?"

The Lord continued to speak with the ease of someone used to command. "Abe, I will make with thee a covenant thou can't refuse. You get all this real estate, no down payment, and as many progeny as careful family planning warrants. In return, every man child and woman child among you shall be circumcised." After asking what circumcision was, and upon being informed, Abe thought: *I knew it sounded too good to be true.*

He got the Lord to drop the custom for women, except for its ritualistic practice among some progressive, lesser-developed nations. Abe didn't fear circumcision himself: *At age ninety-nine,* he reasoned, *I lost all sensation in that area decades ago.* However, explaining it to the less senior men of the tribe was tricky. "It's much more sanitary," he assured them truthfully, and "Women think it's sexy," he attempted. "And it's only fair that men go through some of the same pain of procreation that women in labor endure."

Although Abe was perturbed by the Lord's zest for territorial expansion, he was unfazed by the threat of overpopulation. After all, he was ninety-nine, and Significant Other Sarah was ninety. Sarah had always wanted to dispel the notion it can be dangerous for mature women to have kids; perhaps she had waited a bit too long. Yet neither she nor Abe thought of themselves as overly seasoned, for they were pups compared to figures like Enoch, who lived to be 365, or Methuselah, who reached 969.

Methuselah was the most chronologically enhanced person to ever live, until recent Republican presidential contenders. "I never know what to buy for his birthday," said one of his later spouses. "After receipt of nine hundred plus shaving kits and tool sets, he's truly the man who has everything." The aged but feisty fellow sired offspring until the end of his days; relatives would cluck of his latest mate: "Why, she must be one-fortieth his age. He's elderly enough to be her great-great-great-great-great-great-great-great-great-great-great-great-great-great-great-great-great-great-great-great-great-great-great-great-great-great-great-great-great-great-great-great-great-great-great-great-great-great-great-great-great-great-great-great-great-great-great-great-great-grandfather!"

When he finally passed on, Methuselah had undergone 717 prostate operations. And 256 treatments for gout. After age eighty, a person's health care expenses grow at a logarithmic rate. Methuselah was thus single-handedly responsible for quintupling the rate of health insurance premiums, before the entire system went belly-up. Because of him alone, the retirement age of everyone was raised by thirteen years in a doomed attempt to save people's pensions.

Methuselah was less than spry by his 969th year; when his last spouse was informed he had given up the ghost, she asked, "How could they tell?" Having attended the weddings, bar mitzvahs, and funerals of thousands of friends, Methuselah came to view life as an endless cycle of death and rebirth, and in his seventh century converted to Hinduism.

One hot day, while Abe sat dozing at the flap of his tent, three unusual visitors appeared. Abe somehow sensed the power of the Lord—perhaps it was the wings sticking out of the arrivals' cloaks. After ushering the guests under a shade tree, he offered to wash their feet, but they declined, having flown instead of walked. The host yelled to Sarah, "Make ready quickly three cakes on the hearth," and rushed to fetch the angels milk and butter and to dress a calf's corpse. The visitors were horrified at the atrocious hospitality.

"You should have spared the life of the calf," the first angel lectured Abe. "At least it's suitably dressed, for a decent burial." The second sniffed, "For ethereal beings that weigh nothing at all, we're rather diet-conscious—the butter won't do. Just bring some sesame oil with the cakes, assuming their flour contains no chemical additives."

The third angel chided Abe, "I can't believe you make your spouse do all the cooking. Get thee inside the tent to help with the baking." Desperate to appease their demanding vegetarian guests, Abe and Sarah mashed some young-hen-peas,* squeezed some lemon juice, and invented hummus.

While noshing, the visitors told Abe their next stop was

---

*Chickpeas. The term "chick" is unforgivably sexist.

Sodom, a city famed for helping alienated souls reconnect with their repressed physicality.

"We go there not to rain down fire and brimstone," explained one angel, "but to urge city leaders to decriminalize victimless crimes. If massage therapy, for example, were legalized, Sodom would gain a harmless pastime that yields a steady stream of taxable income."

Soon after, Sarah and Abe finally begat a preadult of their own, named Isaac, or Ike. For almost a century of domestic internment, Sarah had been deemed barren, or so her patriarchal society presumed. (It might have been some deficiency of Abe's.) Abe, a progressive believer in an expansive definition of the family, had fathered his lone preadult with the concubine Hagar.

The previously infertile couple were inspired by the precocious Methuselah. In addition, one of the angels had left a bottle of ginseng in Abe's tent. Further, Abe had heard reports that sperm counts among men had fallen by half, so he tried twice as hard.

When Ike was grown, an aging Abe exposed him to the obscene rite of sacrificial sheep slaughter. Father and son took a torch, butcher knife, and some tree carcass, and rode their donkey companions to a hill, where they built an altar.

Ike innocently asked, "I see the fire and the wood, but what will we use for a burnt offering?"

The 120-year-young Abe replied, somewhat absently, "Ewe."

Ike misheard his dad, and dutifully lay down upon the kindling. When Ike announced he was ready, Abe, somewhat absently, raised up his butcher knife.

Then the Lord spake to Abe, "Lay not thine hand upon thy son. I will bless thee, for thou hast shown me how a ewe must feel when her son is pierced, and later burned to cinders on an altar."

And God placed a regionwide moratorium on sheep incinerations, until suitable prayers were written as a bloodless, substitute way to beseech his favor. The Lord also proscribed the most revolting practice of all, and forbade Middle Eastern restaurants from displaying, for months on end, the same roasted lamb on a slowly rotating spit.

Years later, after extensive counseling, Ike dredged up long-buried memories of the dreadful event, and sued Abe for parental abuse.

# Jake and Esau's Sibling Rivalry

Becky and Ike begat two sons, Jacob and Esau. Although the siblings were twins, they were hardly identical. The hot-tempered Esau had a muscular body matted with red hair, although he may not have been Irish. His hairy, brawny physique clearly suffered from testosterone poisoning. In contrast, the mild-mannered Jake was smooth-skinned. A placid tent-dweller, he preferred staying home with Mom to work on his superior domestic skills. Esau had a severe addiction to stalking and killing non-humans. Overwhelmed by his hunting dependency, he prowled day and night with arrow and bow. After dark, he often bagged motionless deer caught staring at the approach of his servants' torches.

Jake tried to redirect Esau's bloodlust into positive channels. "The main challenge of hunting," he pleaded, "is finding the creature, not causing its premature demise. Why not pack an easel in your quiver and, when chancing upon a deer, paint its picture instead of snuffing out its life?"

Jake also urged his sibling to aim arrows at wooden ducks instead of the real thing. "That's a *canard!*" Esau bristled. "A clever ploy to make me give up my favorite obsession." Jake, anticipating the invention of skeet shooting, even offered to stand at Esau's side and toss waterfowl replicas in the air for the archer to target.

Yet the predator was in denial. "I'm helping maintain the balance of Nature," Esau rationalized. "The deer population is exploding, spilling out onto the roads, with ornery bucks throwing themselves under the wheels of onrushing caravans. Jake, haven't you noticed the amount of roadkill on the trade routes? Don't you know how big a dent a deer puts in a chariot?"

Esau's illicit love for animal flesh had cost him his inheritance. Jake had been puttering around the kitchen one day, trying out recipes with Becky, when Esau had burst in trailing blood over the floor.

"How many times," Jake demanded, hands on aproned hips, "have I asked you to leave your gamy clothes outside?"

"No time for that," blurted Esau. "I've been out stalking all day, and I'm starved!"

Jake asked, "Bet you can't tell the difference between fleshless soup and one with deer carcass."

"Bet I can."

"Bet you can't. But if you're so hensure of yourself, why don't we make a modest wager?"

"Okay, how about my spear for your spice rack?"

"None of that penny-ante stuff. How about this: You guess correctly, and I'll cook any carcass you bring home, without complaint, for forty days and nights. You guess wrong, and I get your birthleft."*

Esau was sure his keen sense of smell, honed by a life of tracking scents, could identify any food. Moreover, he really was famished. His stomach, bloated from years of animal cannibalism, just couldn't say no.

"You're on, Jake!"

Jacob readied two bubbling cauldrons of soup. In one pot he placed a deer carcass. In the other he poured lentils, pungent spices, and a secret ingredient—tofu—that mimicked the disgusting taste of stolen animal flesh without the lethal amounts of sodium and lard. The strong flavorings blocked Esau's vaunted sense of smell. He inhaled the second cauldron's contents before learning he had erred.

Another ruse would worsen Esau and Jake's rivalry.

By the time the siblings were twenty, their birth dad Isaac was almost eighty. Ike was mostly confined to the tent, for he had a pronounced absence of visual acuity. One morning, Jake was preparing a fleshless, eggless, cheeseless, butterless, tasteless breakfast while Esau sharpened arrowheads for the day's massacre. The elderly Ike, his stomach roiling from the prospect of more granola, begged Esau to hunt down some fresh venison. While Jake cringed, Ike said, "Bring me my favorite savory meat and I'll grant you my blessing." Despite a harrowing boyhood experience in which his father Abe had nearly sacrificed him like a lamb, Ike had never developed an aversion to murdered animals. To the contrary he was, like most seasoned males, a meat-and-potatoes myn disdainful of Jake's nouvelle cuisine.

---

*Birthright.

When Rebecca overheard Ike's promise of a prized blessing, she decided to trick Esau again. Becky had always favored Jake; unlike Esau, Ike, or any other male, he'd actually listen to her problems instead of proposing a coldly logical solution. Becky appreciated Jake's underrated contributions to the tent, like his sharp eye for a steep discount at the bazaar. She was incredulous the blessing would go to Esau simply because he was "the oldest," even though the siblings were twins. "Esau happened to be the first out of my womb," Becky fumed, "and he gets all the glory—talk about age discrimination!" (As if intuitively grasping the injustice, Jake had been born clutching Esau's ankle.)

After Esau left to go stalking, Becky told Jake, "Go out to the animal prison yard and get some goat milk. I know it's wrong to rob any creature of its precious bodily fluids, but Ike will expect his nightly mug of warm goat-breast-extract before retiring. As for the snack he so savors, give me the recipe for the lentil soup you foisted on Esau. I'll whip up a batch and you can pass it off on Ike, while you pretend to be Esau."

"Pretend to be Esau?" gasped Jake. "But he's hairy, while I can't even grow a mustache. No matter how visually impaired Dad's become, he'll know it's me when we embrace!"

Undaunted, Becky took dried, hairy goat flesh from Esau's room and tied it to Jake's neck and hands. "Wear this," she directed, "and everything will be fine."

Later that day, Ike took the doctored lentil soup and crept into the quiet room where Isaac sat in darkness.

To compensate for his visual inconvenience, Ike had become more aurally gifted. He heard something approach and asked, "Who or what art thou?"

"I am Esau," stated Jake, giving an alternative version of the truth.

"Parent, here is your disgus . . . your . . . your savory meat pie."

A surprised Ike answered, "How is it thou found a deer so quickly?"

Sweating heavily, his smooth skin scratched by the vile goat remains, Jake tried to imagine how Esau would respond.

"Well, Ike," he hazarded, "you know how the number of prey has exploded lately, what with the tyrannical restrictions on hunting. Deer have been coming clear up to our tent and, finding one just outside, I, I ch-changed her biological classification." Jake gagged at the mere thought of executing an innocent, doe-eyed visitor.

"Here, try this, uh, this yummy soup-with-deer-carcass."

Ike was doubly puzzled, for Esau's voice was higher-pitched than normal. *While out hunting,* he speculated, *was my son kicked in the loins by an equestrian companion? Or is this person an impostor?*

The wary Ike ordered the visitor to formally testify to his identity. In those days, to "testify" meant quite literally that— to hold one's private parts while proclaiming the truth, or issuing a misstatement, whatever the case might be. In a breakthrough for equality of lefts, womyn had just been granted the privilege of holding their private parts in public.

Swallowing hard, Jake testified, misspeaking again that he was Esau, and his voice became even more high-pitched. So much so that, outside the tent, the shepherd dogs howled and strained against their leashes.

The feminine-like voice made Ike more suspicious, so he decided to test the visitor with his keen sense of touch.

"Draw near me, son, and embrace."

So they embraced, and they kissed, for their clan had no repressive taboos on emotional male expression. In fact, they recognized that hugging relieves stress and builds immunity. Ike felt the goat flesh on Jake's neck and hands, and concluded he was Esau and, who knows, maybe he was correct, for truth is relative.

Isaac solemnly blessed Jake, saying:

> *May the road rise up to greet you.*
> *May the wind be always at your back . . .*

Perhaps Ike's son was Irish after all.*

When the benediction was finished, Jake darted from the room as fast as an arrow of Esau's. As soon as he left, Esau entered, announcing, "Let my parent rise, and sup from this scrumptious plate of massacred deer."

Ike trembled exceedingly and thought, *It may be that I'm becoming auditorily and mentally as well as visually challenged.* He asked Esau, "Didn't you bring me something just ten minutes ago?"

Esau's face flushed as crimson as the hair covering his skin. The deceit was swiftly found out. Becky, seeing Esau's wroth, packed Jake off to the land of her relatives. It is unclear whether they were Irish.

---

*The blessing may confirm a widely held belief that the Irish are the descendants of the Lost Tribes of Israel.

oses Faces the Wrath of Pharaokan

For centuries the Israelites dwelt in Egypt, where their merchants opened up mom-and-pop stores in the underprivileged neighborhoods of the Egyptians. They prospered from charging exorbitant prices to unsuspecting shoppers. Protests were staged over the widespread gouging of fiscally disadvantaged customers, as ethnic tensions grew. And the Pharaokan, the Egyptian ruler, said, "The Zionists are conspiring against us. We must be self-reliant, and have native entrepreneurs control their economic destiny." So Pharaokan asked the Israelites to volunteer their services for Egyptian-run construction projects.

Egypt's economy prospered from the resulting public works. Strong worker incentives like twenty-four-hour shifts and public flogging were introduced. To lower employer costs, laborers were paid below the minimum wage, with bread and water. With their own hands the Israelites built many an edifice. "This proves," declared Pharaokan, "they run a Masonic conspiracy of bricklayers to control the world.

"Not that I'm anti-Semitic," he added. "The indigenous pre-Arab peoples of this region are Semites, and I have no problem with them, so by definition I'm not anti-Semitic." Pharaokan thought involuntary servitude a boon under certain conditions, that is, when run by African rulers. He knew non-wage labor has been, along with war, the most inclusive of institutions. Over the ages, everyone's done it: Arab and East Indian traders, American planters, African chieftains, European merchants, Egyptian kings—a mosaic of the world's peoples.

Pharaokan knew the melanin-enhanced skin of his Nation's people absorbed the supercharged rays of the sun god Amon-Ra with great efficiency, far more than the underpigmented. At the same time the people's minds were sharpened by pyramid-shaped hats worn in tribute to their greatest architectural creations. As a result, the Egyptians accomplished more than any civilization since, including a Euro-Western culture that created computers, genetic engineering, and, even more impressively, Post-It notes and TV clickers. In fact, the Eurocentric thinker Aristotle stole all his ideas from the great Egyptian library at Alexandria, constructed two centuries after his demise.

Eons before Columbus invaded Amerika, Egyptian sail people traveled there on boats of papyrus, whose water-resistant properties are evidenced during every rainstorm when splashing pedestrians shield their heads with newsprint. They founded Mexico's purely indigenous Aztec culture, and its pyramid-shaped temples, were indicative—along with widespread human sacrifice—of the benign, all-pervasive Egyptian influence.

To erect their largest building, the Pyramid at Very Elderly Myn—or Geezer—the Egyptians were probably helped by extraterrestrials. By his own account, Pharaokan conversed with the preceding, deceased Pharaoh on board an alien spaceship. Indeed, the Egyptians strongly believed in an afterlife. They lined their burial chambers with tokens of earthly existence to remind them of home when whisked into outer space. The tomb walls held paintings of folks with stiff, oddly contorted arms and legs: Perhaps the Egyptians were not Afrocentrics after all, but melanin-impaired, rhythm-deficient dancers.

The chief challenger to Pharaokan's rule was the Shebrew leader Moses, a member of the Levi tribe who preferred jeans to flowing robes. So, soon after Moses was born, Pharaokan ordered the Israelite midhusbands to terminate with extreme prejudice any newborn males. Citing prejudice of another sort, however, the midhusbands refused to carry out any duties until their exclusively feminine profession was opened up to male nurses. They also denounced the marked gender bias in Pharaokan's order, which singled out males for liquidation while ruling out participation by female infants.

"With all due respect to the Pharaokan," said one midhusband, "his decree is distressingly ageist as well, for it only targets the newborn. Seasoned and middle-elderly people are excluded." A modest proposal was made to eventuate people of every gender and age-group in exactly the same proportion. The Egyptian ruler waxed impatient, however, and ordered every newborn male Israelite tossed into the Nile.

The mother of Moses tried hiding her son, but during his morning bath he'd part the soapy waters of his basin with a wave of his hand, creating a neighborhood sensation in which throngs of the curious crowded into the washroom. A desperate

Ms. Moses rushed down to the Nile's cowrushes and reeds, and launched her son upon a basket fashioned from the same sturdy papyrus used to sail to Amerika. When a scouting party of troops happened by, she became the first person ever to foil pursuers by hiding under water while breathing through a hollow reed. Later Pharaokan's daughter rescued the infant and had Ms. Moses serve as nanny; the latter staged a work stoppage over her society's refusal to let males serve as wet nurses.

When Moses reached adulthood, he wed one of the seven daughters, instead of a son, of the rustic Jethro, a Sinai hill-billy. Jethro was both a sheep prison warden and a priest, and a progressive priest at that, for he evidently played fast and loose with his vow of celibacy. One day Moses, ever watchful for escaped prisoners, was guarding Jethro's ewes when a deity appeared to him in a burning bush. The entity was environmentally aware, for her flame emitted much light but no heat, and did not consume the plant matter.

"I am the Goddess of thy parent," spoke the flame, "the Goddess of Abe, of Izzie, and the Goddess of Jake, and, just as importantly, the Goddess of their Significant Others." The Lady had remembered her pledge to help the Israelites, after getting sidetracked on intergalactic concerns for four centuries. "Through you, I will deliver the Shebrews to the Promised Land." Moses asked the entity her name. The voice resounded, "I Am That I Am," and Moses realized the Creator was a Buddhist. But he was a Reform Jew, so he didn't mind.

Moses fretted he would not persuade the people to go, for he lacked eloquence, and Dale Carnegie was not an option. So to awe the Israelites, the deity gave Moses a staff which, when thrown to the ground, turned into a serpent companion. A confident Moses gathered all the Israelites to tell them about Goddess. However, when he hurled the staff to the earth, the stick turned into a rooster. The Supreme Being had given Moses a defective staff!

A chagrined Moses, his face redder than a burning bush, picked up the squawking bird as feathers swirled about his beard, and the rooster turned back into a staff. His sibling Aaron asked, "Can one ask the Creator for a recall?"

"Buyer beware," replied Moses, who again threw down the rod, and the people guffawed when it yielded a camel. "What do I do, grasp its hump?" Moses cried, and when he grabbed the dromedary it again became a rod.

"Let me try, let me try!" demanded Aaron, and Aaron—after smacking several round stones far into the distance with the staff—tossed it to the ground. This time the people were moderately impressed, for a snake materialized, albeit defanged.

"Next time you see the burning bush," Aaron counseled Moses, "ask for an asp. Egyptian rulers hate asps."

The next time he saw Goddess, Moses traded in his staff for another with an eternity's guarantee. Then he and Aaron went off to schmooze with Pharaokan.

At the royal palace, the monarch was ringed by cross-armed advisors wearing the traditional Egyptian garb of cloth headdress, embroidered gold linen, and silk bow tie. The ruler of his Nation had just returned from a triumphant foreign tour of vassal states and people's democracies in Cyrenaica, Persia, and Mesopotamia, also known as Libya, Iran, and Iraq. The Pharaokan told Moses, "First-name informality is the rule among Egypt's rulers, as King Tut proved. Call me Louie."

"Thanks, call me Mo. My sibling Aaron goes by Hank."

"What can I do for you?"

"Saith the Lady Goddess of Israel, 'Let my peoples go.' I emphasize the plural," said Moses, "for 'people' is noninclusive, and might be misinterpreted to mean the exclusion of Egyptians. In fact, your folks are welcome to come along, if

they don't mind giving up their lush river valley for forty years
of starving in the desert."

At a minimum, Moses sought for his peoples a three-day
retreat in a desert bioregion. Jewish Persons were just beginning a tradition of sending their youths to summer camp, and
a long weekend seemed a prudent way to test out the still-
unproven custom. "And after three days, if we feel like it, we
may just take off for the Promised Land."

"But if the Shebrews leave," noted Pharaokan, "neighborhood stores will be run by new arrivals from Korea, and ethnic tensions will be worse than ever. Request denied."

Moses defiantly hurled his staff to the palace floor, and the
staff turned into a gecko; Pharaokan's rigidly watchful retinue
exploded in mirth. "Close," remarked Aaron. "It *is* a reptile."
Moses gingerly pinched the gecko, and it turned into a staff,
and Aaron took the stick to swing it when Moses restrained
him and led them out of the palace.

"It's just not sensitive," Moses told Aaron, "for us to
pluck some unsuspecting reptile out of her natural abode and
drop her into a hostile, unfamiliar setting." Moses went back
to the burning bush, traded in the rod again, and told the Lady
to conjure up something more persuasive.

Goddess rose to the challenge and unleashed ten plagues.*
In one disturbance, swarms of frogs covered the land. And
frogs are lovers of diversity, for they neither stay strictly on the
land, nor inhabit only the water, but move freely back and
forth between the twain. On another occasion, Moses visited
Pharaokan to warn of a ferocious hailstorm if he didn't relent.

"What's hail?" asked the potentate of the semitropical
kingdom. After Moses' explanation, he opined, "My sun-

---

*Those offended by the word "plague," a speciocentric word with negative con-
notations toward insects, microbes, and unusual weather patterns, may substitute
the term "act of Nature."

drenched people will enjoy the cool, refreshing new weather sensation." When the storm struck, Egyptians did savor the novel taste of crushed-ice drinks. Yet the normally low-maintenance streets of the dry desert country buckled and cracked from the cold, and the tons of Saharan sand thrown onto the roads for traction made things worse. The cold snap even broke off the noble nose of the Sphinx.

Pharaokan was unmoved, so the Lady Goddess brought forth three straight days of darkness. Exactly nine months later, Egypt recorded a record number of births. The baby boom dominated the country's politics for a generation. Despite the steamy liaisons it provoked, the plague of darkness was acutely insensitive to a culture that literally worshipped the sun.

The hail and dearth of sun convinced Pharaokan that, contrary to Noah's experience, the world faced a crisis of global *cooling*. In an emergency address to the Nation, he noted that palms are notorious heat sinks, and asked all matriotic Egyptians to cut down a tree. He urged his countrypeople to hold as many open-air barbecues as possible. He raised subsidies to breeders of oxen, for their herds counteract global cooling with massive emissions of warm methane gas.

In two other acts of Nature, swarms of fly and locust companions engaged in insect community food gathering, and gobbled up every fruit and vegetable. Pharaokan was reduced to eating animal flesh, and he hardened his heart, that is, his arteries, which made him more peevish toward the Israelite demands.

"Some of these plagues are discriminatory," he angrily noted. "In the plague on cattle, Goddess spared the Israelite herds while felling those of the Egyptians. She also passed over the Israelites in smiting the Egyptians' firstborn, and the Egyptians weren't invited to the accompanying Passover ceremonies."

"The Shedrinks'* religious celebration," the head of Egypt's Consumer Protection Agency warned, "entails consumption of unleavened bread with minimal nutritional value."

After this last outrage, Pharaokan let the Israelite people go, but the Egyptians soon missed the Jewish Persons. Lines grew outside the offices of the few remaining dentists, and stand-up comics disappeared from the casbahs. Construction starts plummeted from the departure of the uncompensated laborers from the public works.

To capture the Israelites, Pharaokan relied solely on his land forces, confidently leaving behind the transcontinental gliders and death rays that Egyptian science invented millennia before the West. He rode off from his palace with six hundred equine companions and an equal number of chariots. Sadly, U-shaped leg irons had been thoughtlessly nailed into the companions' hooves. However, as most drivers were emaciated from the plagues, the equines had to haul much less weight than usual.

The vaunted army encountered many delays. Egypt enforced strict speed limits, and police cited many chariots for going too fast. Single drivers were pulled over for traveling in high-occupancy vehicle (HOV) lanes, whose use was required during rush-hour periods like military maneuvers. Most drivers were let go without a ticket, however—the plagues had so depleted the ranks that only one soldier could be spared for each chariot.

While the charioteers tracked their foe, Goddess masked the Israelites with a pillar of smoke. When Moses learned the Egyptians were reeling from the effects of secondary smoke inhalation, he called on the Lady to impose a no-smoking zone

---

*Hebrews. The term "brew," a weakly regulated industrial process that produces massive volumes of perilously alcoholic potables, may be avoided. The gender-preferred form of this word is "Shedrinks."

on herself. After a profuse apology, she banished the noxious pillar, and cloaked the Israelites with a more conventional but equally effective sandstorm. At night, their way was lit by a pillar of fire from clean-burning natural gas.

The opposing sides neared the Red Sea, most of which was actually a Sea of Reeds wetlands preserve. Moses had obtained year-round park passes for the Israelites, who passed through without having to pay. The charioteers had to stop for the entrance fee, and then were shunted onto back-country horse trails that cracked the axles of their vehicles. The Egyptians did approach an Israelite straggler, who became the second person to foil pursuers by hiding under water while breathing through a hollow reed.

To boost the morale of his troops, Pharaokan delivered an inspirational speech, which he claimed One Million Myn attended. The park service, however, estimated the crowd at only twelve hundred, including the equestrian companions. Another delay ensued as Pharaokan sued the park for conspiring to underestimate the crowd size.

After leaving the Sea of Reeds, the Israelites were blocked by an inlet of the Red Sea as Pharaokan's damaged chariots crept ever closer. The trapped Shebrews savaged Moses for not having stayed in Egypt to admire the unmatched tourist attractions and munch contentedly on frogs' legs. The prophet stood on a rise and nervously raised his latest, untested staff over the waves. Nothing happened. He waved the staff again and the waves were unperturbed. At that instant the Egyptian army clattered to the edge of the Israelite host.

As Pharaokan raised his arm to signal an attack, an official from Egypt's Department of Mechanical Vehicles galloped up. The bureaucrat demanded the immediate recall of the defective chariot force. Laboratory tests indicated that, along with defective axles, the razor-like blades protruding from the wheels could snap off and unintentionally smite an opponent.

Pharaokan dismissed the chariots after ordering the riders

to dismount and attack the Israelites on foot, or otherwise if skilled at handstands and tumblesaults. Meanwhile Moses, to his people's profound relief and amazement, got his staff to work. The waters of the Red Sea parted, and Israelites began slipping into Birkenstocks to stroll on across. Pharaokan witnessed Moses' dazzling display of power and wondered, *Would undergoing circumcision be* that *painful?* The sight of an entire ocean bay split in two was as awe-inspiring as a Cecil B. DeMille movie. It was a Kodak moment. "My sibling," said Aaron proudly, "is one helluva mensch."

But Moses' resolve weakened when he saw the schools of fish left floundering on the sea bed. He knew he was responsible for their discomfiture, and for disrupting the feeding patterns of fish trapped on one side or the other of the waterless chasm. He lowered his staff and, greatest miracle of all, his rod worked for a second straight time, and the walls of water crashed back on each other.

"Moses, what have you done? Now we're trapped!" cried the people. But Moses said, "Be patient." And behold, the Red Sea waters receded, and the bay drained, and became a shallow pool that allowed human transit without harming the permanent residents.

Moses explained that Pharaokan had been correct about global climate change. "Planetary cooling expands the polar ice caps," he observed, "and makes sea levels drop sharply all over the world." The joyful Israelites sloshed and schlepped onto the Promised Land. The Egyptians, their fertile Nile Delta tripled in size by a shrinking Mediterranean, gave up war for richly rewarding careers in organic farming.

As for the Pharaokan, he softened his heart and his arteries by giving up meat and race-baiting too. The ruler boarded one of Egypt's papyrus ships and sailed to the Caribbean, where he took up his first love—calypso singing.

# The Ten Recommendations

After fleeing Egypt, the Israelites trekked into the Sinai, crossing over from Africa into Asia. For an odd moment, Moses thought the people seemed more yellowish in hue, more entrepreneurial and respectful of their ancestors, and considerably less vertically advantaged—then the moment passed. At the boundary, whimsical travelers posed for friends with one foot planted in either continent. The Shebrews were to wander the Sinai desert, a compact coastal peninsula, for forty years. They grew dizzy less from the incessant heat than from walking in continuous circles. When queried, Moses said he was "taking an alternate route," but in fact he was directionally challenged. Before setting out, the Israelite leader should have taken a course in asianeering!*

Moses claimed to suffer from a temporal dysfunction, or lateness addiction, but the real trouble lay in the Israelites' patriarchal domination. Typical men, Moses and sibling Aaron were too stubborn to ask for directions.

"It's really not that hard to figure out," commented Miriam, whose gyrating, celebratory dance at the Egyptians' defeat had sparked a *macarena* craze at wadis everywhere. "Sun rise, sun set," the Jewess musician told the tribal chieftain, "sun rise, sun set; and it rises in the east, Moses, which is the direction we want, so head off that way." But Moses had hardened his heart, and as his pre-Arab neighbors wouldn't popularize the compass and astrolabe for centuries thence, more fruitless wandering passed.

"We seek the land of Canaan," he told the people, "not the land of *Caning*: The place we want is also far to the east, but not as far as Singapore."

Instead of toppling Moses and making the levelheaded Miriam boss, the Israelites swallowed hard and adjusted to the clime. Although the Sinai's UV count was dangerously high, its air quality index was invariably a pleasant code green. "One hundred forty degrees in the shade of a palm tree may sound hot," Aaron told Moses, "but people forget there's no humidity." The warm weather and cloudless sky prompted many Israelites to plan on retiring there—and after forty years of wandering, most were well past retirement age. In fact, the Sinai stay began a hallowed Jewish custom in which seniors relocate to a sunny locale with plenty of beachfront property.

Although pleased with their tans, the Shebrews chafed at a

---

*Orienteering. "Orient," a Eurocentric term for relatively more eastern lands, may be replaced with the indigenous term Asia.

chronic want of food and drink—some felt Moses took the anorexic lifestyle too far. Goddess had Moses tap a rock with the hooked rod of tree carcass that had so confounded the Egyptians, and quenching fluid bubbled forth. But the fickle Israelites complained the water wasn't bottled. "What will they want next?" complained Moses. "Tamper-proof caps?" He called the spring Massah, for the water was cool, and the musical Miriam sang a verse of "Massah in da Cold, Cold Ground."

Moses' hypertension worsened as the tribe entered the Rustic Abode for Free-Roaming Non-Human Animals of Ethically Different Behavior, or Wilderness of Sin. His famished folk tightened their belts and girded their loincloths and longed for the foodstuffs of Egypt. The cry rang out: "What I wouldn't give for a locust sandwich!" Husbands stuck for four decades with the scanty kitchen fare of the same woman drooled with fond remembrance of Nile flesh pots.

The people murmured against Moses, who sat on the edge of camp and heard them whisper, "Murmur, Moses, murmur, Moses, murmur, Moses, murmur." He tore at his clothes—and felt cooler in the Sinai heat—and cried out for help to Goddess, who gave him breathing exercises to relieve the strain. "Clear your mind," the Lady instructed. "Then take a long deep breath, and exhale slowly. It works for me."

Moses tried to decompress, but still his people hungered, until one dawn they gazed at the sky—and bagels fell from heaven. Dozens of bagels, of every tint, Benetton-like in their diversity—black and brown and blueberry and strawberry and poppy and mommy, even sesame bagels for the native pre-Arab peoples. The Israelites scooped up the treats, and ate them while perusing the *Sinai Sun* every morn, and were sated. But still not satisfied, for again they murmured against Moses: "Is he sure these things are kosher?" "Some big spender—pastry with holes in the middle," "Bialys are better," and "What, no chives with the cream cheese?"

"That's 'graven images,'" Goddess corrected, "like a statue of a Golden Calf."

"What about craven images?"

"You raise an important point about pornographic material. My feminist side wants to ban exploitation of the female body, while my civil libertarian side deems any restrictions tyrannical—the other third of my Trinity could go either way. An acceptable compromise might lie in limiting craven images to Sodom and Gomorrah."

Moses warily studied the tablets. "These laws make great sound bites, Lady, but my people will never accept them." He shrugged. "It's not like ethics can be written in stone."

"What would you recommend?"

"A more participatory approach. Instead of just telling people what to do or, Heaven forbid, setting a moral example, you should ask them what they want."

"I can read the mind of everyone on Sinai."

"I'd suggest a more scientific approach: Conduct polls and focus groups of the Israelites, and tailor your suggestions to their views. Popular deities tell the people exactly what they want to hear."

Moses volunteered, in exchange for a consulting fee, to conduct the opinion surveys. He gathered groups of what he called "undecideds"—people willing to entertain the existence of Goddess but wary of religious ritual or theological disputes. He test-marketed the revised recommendations through questionnaires, which included the following Q & A:

Q: "Is it socially acceptable to take the name of a god in vain?"

A: "It depends. Swearing is generally not a valid substitute for a finely articulated statement of position. But it can relieve stress, or convey to the listener the seriousness of the curser's opinion."

THE POLITICALLY CORRECT GUIDE TO THE BIBLE  67

Q: "Is someone who commits adultery, or preadultery, ethically impeded?"

A: "It depends, but probably not. He, she, we, or it is likely striking a blow for personal liberation and the end of repressive marital institutions."

Based on Moses' findings, the Lady released the nonbinding set of suggestions below, which are revised slightly to reflect modern sensibilities:

## THE TEN RECOMMENDATIONS*

1. *Thou shalt treat all gods, goddesses, demigods, demigoddesses, cults, and beliefs with equal respect and devotion.*

2. *Thou shalt honor thy birth mother or birth father, or mother and father of step, or mother and mother or father and father, or surrogate mom or surrogate dad. Or thou shalt sue any of the above for negligence. Although honoring one's household guardians is acceptable, remember: It takes a village.*

3. *Thou shalt not steal, except when:*

- *Charging $2 for an ATM transaction.*

- *Robbing defenseless seniors in disadvantaged areas, as the income redistributor is likely the unwitting victim of unremitting social and economic conditions.*

---

*The Recommendations are numbered for convenience; no offense is intended proponents of lettered as opposed to numbered lists. Readers are free to imagine a dashed list if they like. Because it evokes gun violence, a bulleted list was avoided. (Because structured lists imply the possibility of meaning, deconstructionists and other literary scholars may scramble the text into an indecipherable jumble.)

*Stealing will be universally ignored when limited to paper clips and memo pads taken from the office supply cabinet.*

4. *Thou shalt commit adultery, or preadultery: If it feeleth good, do it. Particularly if you're French, and keeping a mistress or manstress is expected. Or the insatiable governor of a southern state whose troopers tempt him with an endless supply of willing consorts. Or a leading legislator with a spouse recovering from cancer. Or a member of the royal family. However, thou shalt in every circumstance avoid the appearance of impropriety.*

*Under pain of death, no man shall grab, touch, make advances to, talk to, comment on the apparel of, look at, or think about a woman.*

5. *The most important recommendation is: Thou shalt not discriminate on the basis of religion, race, agnosticism, atheism, national origin, sexual preference, gender or genders, marital status, parental status, income (unless affluent), age, youth, ability, accent, preexisting medical conditions, future medical conditions, pregnancy status, culture, lack of culture, test scores, appearance, scent, political affiliation (if the approved kind), veteran's status, draft-dodging status, citizenship, planetary origin, drug test results, species, or ethics.*

*Thou shalt discriminate in the preferential award of housing, college admissions, and high governmental positions. The above rules supersede the prior, overly simplistic, and insufficiently bureaucratic and legalistic rule: "Do unto others as you would have them do unto you."*

6. *Thou shalt not be factually challenged nor engage in an excess of literalism nor otherwise bear false witness, unless plea bargaining, or campaigning for or holding office.*

*7. Thou shalt not worship false idols, Elvis excepted.*

*8. Thou shalt not diss, unless you can afford a Dream Team of morally disengaged attorneys. Other myriad exceptions include: wars, crusades, jihads, assisted suicides, intact dilation and evacuation during the terminal stages of the third trimester, and capital punishment.*

*9. Thou shalt remember the Sabbath Day, so thou can get all thy shopping done at that time. No establishment in a mall shall be shuttered any hour of the week. Everyone will work three jobs to make ends meet.*

*10. Thou shalt not take the name of God in vain, but with gusto, particularly if a gangsta rap artist or Roseanne, lest any verbal restraint have a chilling effect on free speech. However, all offensive speech shall be banned in the workplace and on college campuses.*

*The unofficial, eleventh recommendation is:*
*Thou shalt never place the original Ten Commandments on a schoolhouse wall.*

Pleased with the revamped Recommendations, the Lady asked Moses to house them in a specially constructed Ark of the Covenant. "In all our years in the Sinai," Moses replied incredulously, "it's only rained twice. I didn't even bring a slicker."

"Not Noah's kind of ark." She chuckled. If Moses built a tabernacle, the Lady promised, he would get a New Covenant of middle-class tax cuts, health care reform, and a government free of ethical misconduct.

When Moses returned from the mountain top, he saw the

people had crafted a Golden Calf. The idol was an unsurpassed expression of artistic skill and religious devotion. On the verge of a new land, the Israelites understandably wished to share the customs of the Native Peoples and the nonhuman animals they worshipped. So they shopped around the different cults to pick and choose between monotheistic and pagan rites. As Miriam remarked, "After an endless tramp through a desert, I understand how the Egyptians could come to worship the sun or the Nile's reviving waters." As Aaron succinctly put it, "When in Canaan, do as the Canaanites do."

Striding genially into camp, a tanned, rested Moses tossed aside the tablets of the original recommendations, declaiming, "We won't be needing these!" Regarding the Calf, he shared the general sentiment. "It's nice to see a four-legged creature placed at the core of our normally human-centered beliefs. And the preadult subject of a calf is a pleasant contrast to the grown-up authority figures usually found in public statuary."

However, the large quantity of bullion gave Moses pause. *The sudden withdrawal of so much gold from the public purse could trigger a sharp deflationary spiral,* he worried. *And if the Calf were melted down, the sudden influx of bullion could spark hyperflation.* Then he felt a sudden wave of hunger after his six-week fast, and eagerly joined those feasting around the metal shrine.

When the multicultural celebration was done, the Israelites decamped for the Region of High-Protein Byproducts Stolen from Voiceless, Defenseless Bovine Companions and High-Energy, High-Calorie Nectar Unjustly Appropriated from Innocent-But-Hardly-Defenseless Buzzing Insects.*

---

*The Land of Milk and Honey.

# Joshua's New Age Army

Mighty Jericho was a gated community. Its security force of armed warriors carefully checked anyone entering or leaving its towered walls. Few residents ventured outside for fear of having their transportation horse-jacked. The well-protected city was a formidable obstacle for the Shebrew leader Joshua. His siege of the heavily fortified town would have been tough enough without the army reforms he had to administer. "Our nomadic calvary vexes me," Joshua complained. The Israelite military was under intense pressure to hire more Bedouins, who enlisted not so much to see the world (they were already far-roaming travelers), but for the steady work. A court order had made the number of nomads in Joshua's military equal to their proportion of the general population.

"They're a fierce and courageous people," he readily admitted, "although the charge of their camels won't set any speed records. But what really annoys me is their habit of wandering off at the crucial moment of a battle—not out of cowardice, but due to the urge to roam."

The placement of females in combat units raised other concerns. Because of the prolonged siege of Jericho, some armchair conservatives feared the women would get infections from sitting in trenches, although the region's pervasive dry heat alleviated this concern. Many did become pregnant, however, from sharing the trenches with men. When traditionalist officers threatened to resign over their new recruits, Joshua compromised with a "Don't Ask, Don't Tell" policy in which women were allowed to serve—as long as they didn't tell anyone they were women.

Joshua thought it ungrateful of the new lady officers, who had yet to experience combat, to complain about having a smaller percentage of combat medals than males. He was annoyed when, citing the train of camp followers who followed the armies of the time, the women demanded equal access to male harlots.

"And my male drill instructors!" Joshua groaned. "They spend more time dating enlistees than getting them into shape."

The recruitment of soldiers of alternative gender preference brought more dramatic changes. Most armies laid waste to the cities they seized; towns the new soldiers occupied experienced a commercial boom and cultural renaissance. Drab barracks were transformed into attractive town houses.

The army's corps of engineers was renamed the army corps of landscape architects.

The new soldiers rebelled over their tasteless rations, and demanded gourmet mess kits. They rejected their ill-fitting field tunics and wore impeccably tailored dress uniforms into battle. Instead of going out on maneuvers, some units now preferred to be choreographed.

Joshua also faced the matter of "gold-plating" among his defense contractors. Taking advantage of regulations that required the rarest, most expensive materials in military hardware, profit-hungry firms had built an ultrasophisticated, next-generation war chariot for the eye-popping cost of 220 billion shekels. The solid gold vehicle could outmaneuver and outfight any rival contraption, and it had such superb suspension that rabbis could perform circumcisions in it while bouncing along rutted country roads. However, its great expense limited its production volume—to a single chariot.

Joshua's request for a mass production run of two chariots, which could be constructed for the bargain price of 100 billion shekels a piece, gathered dust. He was stuck with a situation in which a single broken wheel would unhinge his entire mechanized force. For fear of damage to the vehicle or capture of its priceless technology by the enemy, Joshua ordered it placed in permanent reserve.

Still, a way was found to carry the fight to the enemy. In a bold espionage scheme, Joshua slipped his most trusted advisor—"Mo" Morris—into Jericho, where he stayed at the house of a two hundred-shekel-an-hour harlot. As the aide's feet were blistered from endless campaign marches, the sex entrepreneur stroked his fetish for anointing and washing the pedal extremities. As a token of gratitude, the advisor shared with the harlot private communications from the Israelites' commander-in-chief.

When the scribes of Jericho uncovered the steamy affair

and published Joshua's missives, the mortified top Israelite fired his aide and launched a futile attack on Jericho to divert media coverage from the scandal. Far from feeling ashamed, the advisor and victimless-crime proponent were elated over their newfound notoriety, which they exploited by writing bare-all best-sellers.

"I work the world's oldest profession," bragged the harlot in the introduction to her screed. "And I," bragged the shifty politico in his intro, "work the world's second-oldest, with a job description identical to the first."

Plagued by scandal and glitches in assimilating the female and nomad forces, Joshua almost despaired of seizing Jericho. Then he devised the famous strategy of musical encirclement.

Joshua assembled his army and announced, "You will march around Jericho's walls each day for a week." A soldier asked, "But won't we get dizzy? At least let us vary the march, and go in one direction one day, and in the other direction the next."

The commynder-in-chief agreed and said, "Seven priestesses carrying ram's horns will lead the procession."

A nomad asked, "But doesn't that violate separation of church and state, with the church infringing upon the state's war-making prerogative?"

Joshua replied, "The use of prayers, chaplains, and priestesses has ample precedent, and is sanctioned by the courts." He added, "On the seventh day we'll march seven times around the city."

A priestess asked, "But isn't the seventh day the day of rest? Doesn't that violate separation of church and state, with the state infringing upon a synagogue's prerogative of ministering devotional services?"

A soldier responded, "I believe Josh means the seventh day in a general sense, and not necessarily the sabbath. But I'm more concerned about the ram's horns the priestesses carry. They're a blatant symbol of traditional sex roles and male aggressiveness."

The substition of ewes' wool for rams' horns was put up to a voice vote of the democratically run army, and narrowly defeated, when Joshua noted the whole purpose of the stratagem was to blow the horns.

The daily marches began, with routes alternating every morning. On the third day, Joshua was savoring lunch from his gourmet mess kit when a messenger ran up.

"Sir, we've just lost half our army."

"Did the nomads bolt again?"

"No, two of the four corps commanders declared themselves free agents, and took their troops with them."

"Free agency," Joshua sighed, "has become the bane of our highly competitive profession." Often in midbattle, yea, even in mid–sword thrust, a prized warrior would switch sides and go with the highest bidder. Wily agents roamed opposing camps and enticed underpaid, unappreciated soldiers to play for the other flag.

"There's just no loyalty to city or nation anymore," Joshua complained to the courier. "Not like when I was growing up, when a loyal core of hardened veterans would stay with the same squad through retirement, or until carried out on their shields. I tell you, I don't even know who's the starting phalanx for the Hebrew Nationals anymore. You need a scorecard to tell which side a spear chucker is on." Joshua lured the commanders back with a ten-year, no-cut contract plus incentives, such as permission to keep any loot taken from Jericho.

On the seventh day, which was not necessarily the sabbath day, the seven priestesses with the seven rams' horns circled Jericho with the richly compensated, free-agent army. Joshua had ordered everyone's ears stuffed with stolen lambs' hair. He gave a prearranged signal, and the trumpets blared a baleful refrain—"Feelings." The terrified citizens of Jericho covered up their ears, but couldn't block the sickly-sweet melody. They sued for peace (everything had become susceptible to legal action) and, on Joshua's order, leveled their proud towers.

The psych-ops, or psychological operations tactics, had been a resounding success.* The city of Jericho applied for urban renewal assistance.

Joshua moved quickly to follow up his smashing victory by marching against the Amorites, but darkness threatened to cloak his fleeing opponents under cover of night. Night-vision goggles had yet to be devised for desert wars.

So Joshua called out, "Sun, stand thou still, and thou Moon, stay in the valley." And the sun stood still, and the moon stayed, and the commander's victorious troops marveled, saying, "That Joshua fellow has some chutzpah."

The Israelites seized the lands formerly occupied by the Hittites, Amorites, and Canaanites. All still have claims pending before the World Court.

More important than the conquests were the unintended consequences of the celestial interventions. Merchants were late for appointments because their sundials got stuck on the same shadow. Sunburnt farmers fainted from prolonged solar exposure; crops withered and waterholes dried up. As in the hottest times of the summer, rates of murder and violent assault rose.

The diurnal rhythms of countless animals were disrupted, and nocturnal creatures went hungry waiting for the setting sun. The temporary suspension of the moon's phasing process was grossly unfair to maritime denizens dependent on the lunar tides. If Mars had fragile microscopic life at that time, as is likely, the solar transformation may have eradicated it, as well as ending life on other planets.

"Never," Joshua concluded, "mess with Mother Nature."

---

*Thus began a military tradition, extending to the invasions of Panama and Waco, Texas, of aiming loud, offensive music at hostile compounds.

# Samdaughter and Delilah

Samdaughter—or Samanthadaughter, or Samanthason, or Samson—was a fellow with immense strength and great hair. His follicular endowment, like his Herculean physique, would have made Fabio jealous. Each day he spent hours pumping bronze (the Iron Age was still a few centuries off), without neglecting the low-impact aerobics vital to maintaining cardiovascular health. He further boosted his strength by placing an adhesive strip across his nose. The hirsute bodybuilder was sexually active, and frequented Philistine harlots in Gaza, at the infamous

"Gaza Strip." Because of his athletic prowess, full head of hair, and affection for shiksas, it was hard to believe he was Jewish.

Once while out in the country trolling for sex objects, a lion attacked him. *I could wring his neck in an instant,* Samdaughter thought, *but I'm the culprit here, intruding on his ecological niche.* So the strong myn fled, and tried clambering up a fig tree, but was too muscle-bound to climb very far before the quick cat was upon him. Thus, he clamped the maw with one massive hand and gently squeezed the throat with the other until the lion passed out. Samdaughter cared for the cubs until their daddy started to stir.

Samdaughter's pacifism ebbed when he learned about the Philistines' illicit agriculture. Their cornfields, vineyards, and olive groves formed the basis of dangerously alcoholic drugs: Corn for moonshine, grapes for wine, and olives for martinis.

"We can't trust the people to make correct decisions about consuming such vile potions," concluded Samdaughter, "so we must outlaw these substances."

Acting on his beliefs, he tied together the tails of three hundred sex objects, or foxes, thrust a flaming torch into each knot, and drove the highly intelligent, highly attractive, and highly flammable creatures through the Philistine estates, consuming all in a cleansing fire.

Growers angered by the ruined produce, and no longer able to appease their sorrows in soothing libations, contrived to capture their tormentor. They approached Delilah, a visual harassment survivor who'd lost her waitron job at the Chest Fever chain of oasis eateries. Chest Fever was furiously downsizing female waitrons and hiring males in response to a suit over its all-womyn service staff. Delilah knew Samdaughter in the biblical sense of the word.

"Find out how to foil his awesome strength," the Philistines offered the underemployed femme fatale, "and one thousand taels of grains will be yours."

"What's a tael?" asked Delilah. When informed it meant a large quantity, she answered, "Sorry, cash or credit only."

The following Saturday night, Samdaughter and Delilah lolled on her satin bedcovers, with the estrogen-charged temptress pinching the he-myn's pecs and rustling his spectacular locks. Behind the bed curtain, a phalanx of armed Philistines waited expectantly.

"Sammy," she cooed, "we've had a relationship for what must have been days, but I know nothing about you. I've related my innermost secrets, but you don't emote anything to me."

"All us guys are like that," Samdaughter regretted. "We'll argue for months over which javelin hurler has the best throwing arm, but never spill our guts over stuff that really matters. I need to find the courage to change, and learn to share my feelings."

"You might start," said Delilah hopefully, "by confiding to me the secret of your strength. I know it isn't steroids. Tell me, how could you be tied up and rendered helpless?" Behind the curtain, the Philistines put down their swords, and took out stylus and papyrus to mark Samdaughter's words.

"I'd be defenseless," the Israelite grinned, "if bound with seven willow stems."

"Thou mockest me!" Delilah shot back. "Even very seasoned Methuselah at age nine hundred could burst a bundle of stems."

"I'll level with you, Delilah. What really slays me is being bound with chains."

The eavesdropping Philistines made careful note, and sent off to Gomorrah for a rush delivery of bedroom chains. Delilah bound Samdaughter's hands and chest with the metal, and interacted with her mate, and Samdaughter fell asleep—as noncommunicative males are wont to do after such interactions.

Delilah shouted, "The Philistines are upon thee, Samdaughter!" and the Israelite, startled awake, burst the chains about his chest with a mere inhalation, and broke the links about his hands with a twist of the wrists. He effortlessly crushed the Philistines, who had forgotten to exchange styli for swords, and tossed his foes in a heap upon the floor. During the free-for-all, Samdaughter wielded his preferred weapon, the jawbone of a derriere.

"Thou hast mocked me," said Delilah, "and misstated the facts," and Samdaughter almost shouted, "You should talk!" but held his tongue, for he was still hesitant to bare his most intimate feelings.

Delilah calmed down by visualizing the hefty payment due her. Sidling up to Samdaughter again, she breathed, "Tell me, Sammy, how could you be tied up and rendered helpless?" Behind the curtain, a replacement phalanx of Philistines took up position with trepidation, and took out stylus and papyrus.

"What really slays me, Delilah, is being tied up with leather."

The Philistines took meticulous notes, and sent off to Sodom for an express delivery of leather straps. Delilah bound Samdaughter's hands and chest, and he fell asleep after another mutual interaction, and Delilah, unimpressed by the alleged strong myn's stamina, shouted, "The Philistines are upon you, Samdaughter!" The Israelite found the leather bindings a cinch after the metal chains, and burst them, and heaped the floor further with the cerebrally underutilized Philistines, who again forgot to pick up their swords.

On every night of the following week, Delilah expressed to Samdaughter her innermost feelings in a most emotive way, a technique known as "nagging," and even a fellow with Samdaughter's considerable reserves of strength was worn down, his soul vexed unto death. Meanwhile another group of Philistines trembled behind the curtain, this time tightly gripping their swords.

Exhausted by his consort's verbal harassment, Samdaughter succumbed.

"You win, Delilah. Against every instinct of my sex, I will make an emotional commitment, and tell you my secret. To render me helpless, weave the tresses of my hair with the pin of your loom."

"Weave your locks with my loom? You're putting me on again!" she howled.

But Samdaughter insisted, and a dubious Delilah complied, and worked the device that consigned generations of sisters to forgoing careers outside the home. She slipped the loom's pin into the luxurious tresses and, lo, the strong myn's locks drew up from his pate.

Samdaughter was tonsurally challenged.

"Yes, it's true," he rued, "I have a rug. I know it's vain, but without this piece my self-image is abysmal, and I can't face any challenge.

"The follicularly deprived suffer an array of discriminatory practices," he anguished. "Ageism—because we seem more senior, and people think less of the seasoned. And lookism—because people find the hirsute more attractive. . . ."

As if to prove his point, Delilah gave Samdaughter the once-over, and rejoiced in her betrayal. *He could be my grandparent,* she reflected in horror. *Imagine being seen in public with a relic like that!*

". . . And the verbal slurs like 'beacon brow.' The government should treat tonsural deprivation as a disability, Delilah, and provide tax credits for wigs and weaves." Behind the curtain, the all-male Philistine troop sympathized with Sam's all-too-common plight and took a collection for an implant, before recalling their mission.

The soldiers seized the defenseless, spiritually broken Israelite and bound him in a new pair of naughty Gomorrah chains. They made him somewhat visually challenged by plucking out his eyes, which ended his long-standing visual harassment of the treacherous but toothsome Delilah. The former waitron piled on by announcing she was suing her former suitor for palimony.

The distraught he-myn was taken to a rehabilitation center, and he did grind in the prison house, making license plates for chariots. Yet during his stay, a herbalist slipped Samdaughter a potion, the precursor to Rogaine. Magnificent tresses soon covered Samdaughter's forlorn pate, and he regained his self-image. The guards, uncouth Philistines who paid no heed to personal style, didn't notice. Or perhaps they were visually challenged themselves, or simply inattentive.

At length the Philistines held a festival in their temple, and invited Samdaughter to attend. While listening to the fervent pagan rites, the guest came to admire the obviously sincere beliefs. Thus, when a fire broke out in the building, he acted swiftly to save his hosts. The optically constrained body builder groped for the temples' central pillars and pulled them down, opening a hole in the main wall to let the worshippers escape. His mighty shoulders supported the aperture, which threatened to collapse from the fire's heat, until everyone was safely outside. Everyone, that is, except Delilah and her palimony attorney, the latest live-in lover of the ex–Chest Fever waitron. Ignoring their cries for help, Samdaughter stepped outside the temple and the hole collapsed, sealing the doomed couple inside.

Granted a pardon for his heroic deed, Samdaughter worked nights to obtain his law degree, then sued the Israelites for verbal slander. "They have turned the word Philistine," stated his legal brief, "into a common household term of opprobrium." After winning an unanimous verdict before an all-Philistine jury, he was elected judge by his newly adopted people. In his later years, he organized Philistine Awareness Week.

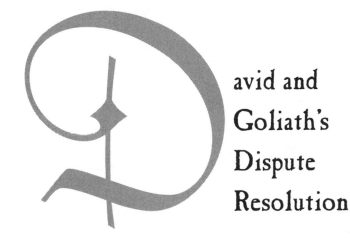

# avid and Goliath's Dispute Resolution

Goliath was strong and very vertically endowed. He stood almost four meters in height and, when dressed for battle, wore a suit of femail that alone outweighed most opponents. Yet despite an impressive build, Goliath was a frustrated, misunderstood individual. From his earliest years, he was the target of heightism, such as the taunts of insensitive schoolmates over whom he towered. He was shunned, apart from being chosen first for games of kickball—so size-enabled was Goliath that he completely blocked the goal just by standing in front of it.

Goliath was also victimized for his differential style of dress. Because of his size, Goliath was unable to find large enough tunics at the local bazaar, and as a result wore undersized clothes that only accentuated his verticality. And later in life, judgmental persons objected to the skulls of slain foes he strung around his neck.

As a preadult, Goliath was very hyperactive. His condition resulted from high blood sugar typical of lads who snacked in the Land of Milk and Honey. A supercharged metabolism forced him, against his will, to pick fights with fellow preadults. In the later stages of preadulthood, Goliath hung with members of an attention-seeking social club that staged ride-by stonings of rival clubs. To prove their valor, tough native youths would steal the hubcaps off chariots— while they were being driven. In medium,* Goliath fell prey to an unnurturing environment and his own uncontrollable impulses.

Goliath was part of an oppressed group of Indigenous Persons, the Philistines. They were waging a successful war of national liberation against their Zionist occupiers, and Goliath was their fiercest fighter. They won battle after battle until the decimated Israelites barely had soldiers for a small peacekeeping mission. Falafel merchants made jokes that Israelite chariots had only one gear, and it went in reverse. Faced with disaster, the Hebrews' King Saul tried a daring gambit to turn the humanpower shortage to his advantage.

Saul decided to settle the destiny of the region with a fight between each side's most skilled warrior. He proposed that

---

*In short. Terms such as "in short" and "at length" may offend humyns who are differentially sized. The term "medium" is not intended to offend fortune-tellers or Gypsy-Americans.

whichever side lost become the slaves of the winning side, and granted health care that was fully transportable upon switching jobs. With the seemingly invincible Goliath as their champion, the Philistines readily accepted the offer.

At that time an Israelite named Jesse had sired, due to ignorance of safe-sex practices, eight sons. The least elderly of the siblings was a poetry student and part-time lyre player named David. One day David was asked by his father, a misguided Zionist, to take a supply of cheese, corn, and bread to the hard-pressed Israelite army.

As a devout vegetarian, David declined to take the cheese, a byproduct of bovine body fluids, and a staple of wishy-washy ovolactovegetarians who accommodate the prevailing flesh-eating ethic by consuming egg and milk products. He also left behind the loaves; David subsisted on pita bread, which he called "Syrian bread" to show he bore no grudge against one of his tribe's sworn enemies. Slinging over his shoulder a small sack of parched corn, David left to feed the Israelite camp.

Upon his arrival David learned about Goliath, and asked King Saul to let him take on the enemy champion. But the reactionary Saul refused to consider the beardless, vertically challenged preadult. His kingdom practiced reverse age discrimination against the less temporally gifted. At a time when brute strength, not PC* skills, determined battlefield success, David's altitudinal disability was also held against him. Further, the poetry student's lack of facial hair was considered "effeminate" by a chest-thumping, male-dominated culture whose prophets and kings had a fetish for long, straggly beards. Enraged at David's impertinent request, Saul hurled a spear at him, but the lithe petitioner dodged the speeding missile.

---

*In this case, PC means personal computer, not political correctness.

Saul demanded of David, "Give me one good, bad, or indifferent reason why you should be champion."

"I've met tough challenges before," David replied. "Once a neighbor was troubled by a burgeoning lamb population that was overgrazing its semiarid land. My solution was to climb a nearby mountain, where I captured a lion and bear after lulling them to sleep with my lyre. Then I released the two nonhuman predators near the lambs, whose numbers have since been kept in check by their natural enemies."

"I've heard of this creature management project," commented Saul. "Haven't the lion and bear mauled some of the shepherds?"

"Yes," said David, "but the matter's being resolved. The shepherds will ask the government for permission to use their staffs in self-defense."

Saul relented and chose David to represent his army. His change in heart was due partly to the shepherd story, partly because he had wrenched his shoulder hurling the spear—and couldn't throw anymore—and partly because nobody else volunteered.

Before the battle, a worried Saul offered David his own weapons and armor, which included a suit of femail. But to the king's chagrin, the preadult declined the royal gift.

"As a weapons-control advocate," David asserted, "I cannot raise a sword against another person, nor provoke an intemperate response from a bloodthirsty maniac by donning threatening armor."

With the kingdom at stake, Saul bid David protect himself and, as a compromise, David agreed to buy a special nonlethal sling. The sling hurled cloth-wrapped "dumdum" stones that merely stun, not smite, a person who happens to violently disagree with the slinger's point of view. A delay in the encounter with Goliath ensued because of the mandatory twelve-day training session that taught David how to safely operate his kinder-and-gentler weapon.

When the fateful day arrived, the two opponents prepared for battle. Goliath strapped onto his ankles mammoth boots made from the cured hides of slaughtered cattle. David, refusing to wear the skin of slain animal citizens, slipped into comfy size-6 sandals fashioned from palmetto leaves. Unlike David, Goliath declined to wear the safety helmet prescribed by law to prevent head injuries. Both men, like most male fighters of that time, wore a skirt or kilt, which leads womyn's studies herstorians to suspect David and Goliath were transvestially inclined.

Goliath showed up heavily armed. Despite local attempts to regulate the purchase of blades, sales of spears and swords were unrestricted in neighboring kingdoms, leading to a vast cross-border traffic in illegal weapons. Although deadly scimitars were banned, Goliath had obtained several on the gray market. A few nations prohibited weapons altogether, but they were invariably wiped out when their defenseless warriors encountered heavily armed enemies disdainful of weapons control.

As the confident Philistine host looked on with anticipation, and the shrunken Israelite force with trepidation, Goliath and David walked into the valley separating the two sides. Goliath moved with a prideful swagger that shook the earth. He hummed to himself: "Yea, though I walk through the valley of death, I shall fear no ethically challenged behavior, for I am bad to the bone." David walked hesitantly, pausing often to ensure he didn't step on any insects. A servant ran over with a broom, and David slowly swept the earth in front of him to prevent any unintended squashings. When the two neared the valley's midpoint, David was careful to keep his distance from Goliath: He wanted his opponent safely out of range of the sling.

Goliath tried intimidating David with a gruesome boast: "I'll feed your rotting flesh to the fowls of the air and the beasts of the earth." But David just smiled, thinking, *Goliath may have a mean streak, but his views on recycling are quite innovative.*

The encounter heated up with a sharp exchange of words on the merits of ordnance control.

"Weapons, not people, are the cause of violence!" affirmed David.

"Swords don't draw themselves out of their sheaths!" Goliath countered.

"We need to sweep spears and daggers off our streets and trade routes," stated David.

Goliath retorted, "Then how are law-abiding cart and camel drivers supposed to defend themselves against the likes of violent thugs like myself?"

"But disarmament is the path to peace."

"Peace through strength!"

"We have to give our opponents the benefit of the doubt."

"Trust but verify!"

"At the very least," pleaded the Israelite, "let's put some limits on the length of blades."

"That's a transparent and cowardly attempt," countered the Philistine, "to disarm me on the verge of battle."

The two champions resorted to slinging personal insults.

"You're a height-disadvantaged preadult of suspect gender," taunted Goliath of his vertically impaired, downy-chinned opponent.

"You're an altitudinally differentiated persun of a verbally expressive nature," David responded to his vertically enhanced, foul-mouthed foe.

To David's shock, this slight reduced Goliath to tears.

"What's the matter?" he asked with concern. "Are you hurt?"

"No," sniffled his theretofore hard-boiled opponent. "It's just that everyone makes fun of my size. Ever since I can remember I've been stereotyped as an oversized lout." And Goliath sobbed some more.

"I know what you're going through," empathized David, his voice cracking with emotion. "I've always been branded 'shorty' and 'squirt.'" And tears fell down the flushed cheeks of the Israelite.

The pitiful sounds of the champions' bawling overwhelmed the already strained nerves of the waiting armies, and every soldier on both sides began to cry. A trickle of tears became a steady falling stream, and then a torrent pouring upon the ground, which collected into rivulets and rivers, and eventually made their way to the Biologically Challenged (Dead) Sea, which remains salty to this day.

David threw down his sling, and Goliath tossed aside his spear, shield, string of skulls, and scimitar. Overcome by their common bond, the champions embraced.

"Back in school," cried David, "when teachers made students assemble by order of height, I was always the very first or very last in line. There was no place to hide: It was psychologically devastating!"

"The same thing happened to early-maturing oafs like myself!" wailed Goliath. "You know, Dave, I've never had a male companion I could open up to." And the Philistine warrior gently wiped away the Israelite's tears with his tunic's blanket-sized sleeve.

"My height disability is such a burden," moaned David. "Sometimes you have to ask a woman, for god's sake, to help you climb onto a donkey. I know that's a gender-insensitive thing to say, but it's true."

"Being altitudinally advantaged is also traumatizing," noted Goliath. "Everyone stares when you stoop to enter a tent designed for the tiny people of these ancient times."

Comforted by their newfound support group, the two victimized persons ceased crying, and walked out of the valley arm in arm. The next morning, they suggested that envoys of the Pharaoh initiate a regional peace process.

The future King David launched a successful career in politics and, on the side, authored a psalms anthology read at coffeehouses from Gaza to Gomorrah. Goliath poured his formidable, aggressive energies into entrepreneurship, and founded the first tall men's clothing store.

# onah's Cetacean Companion

Jonah had finished packing for his long-awaited vacation when the Lord, without warning or salutation, said unto him: "Arise, get thee to Nineveh, for that Sin City is ethically challenged." But Jonah thought, *Oh sure, just drop everything and go. Don't even offer to pick up the tab for my casbah reservations. Nineveh does have a rep as a moral vacuum, but what business of that is mine?* So Jonah went instead to Joppa, to catch his Mediterranean cruise. At the bustling seaport, soldiers were inspecting travel bags—Jonah learned the port had received a threatening note concerning his ship. The missive was unsigned, the anonymous author had written in explanation, because no one, including Himself, was permitted to utter or inscribe His name in public, not to mention taking it in vain.

Seaport officials searched for hidden explosives with the latest technology. Inside the dim light of a tent, a flaming torch threw passengers' shadows against the canvas to reveal suspicious bulges. Suspects were submitted to a strip search (visitors from Sodom *demanded* a strip search), despite the protests of the Area Civil Liberties Union.

Jonah reached the ticket clerk.

"One-way or round trip?" he was asked.

"I've a funny feeling I won't need a return fare."

"Very well, nonsmoking or nonsmoking?"

"Let me see . . . nonsmoking."

"Has any stranger asked you to carry an unidentified package on board?"

"I don't think so."

"Mr. Jonah, would you like to purchase traveler's insurance?"

"What's the premium?"

"Well, to be frank, your name is a synonym for an unlucky person. And you know how superstitious sail persons are, so the premium's stiff."

"I'll skip the insurance."

"Do you have anything to declare?"

"Only that the Lord is encroaching upon my personal space, and that I should have the right to choose my own destination without interference. As for my predestination, that's for the Lord to decide."

Soon after departure, a fierce tempest smote the sea, which wrought and was tempestuous. The shipmistress roped herself to the steering wheel and called out: "I'd like to welcome everyone on board *The Ill-Fated* for today's voyage. The expected sailing time for our trip is indeterminate. I just checked with the copilot, and she expects cyclonic conditions for the balance of the cruise. As we may be experiencing some turbulence, I'd like to recommend folks fasten their sea harnesses. In the event of an unanticipated event, we have two emergency exits: over the port side, and over the starboard.

"And remember, smoking on board is strictly forbidden."

The battered vessel began to list, even though waves had reduced the ballast by sweeping many crew members out to sea. The shipmistress sought a further reduction by ordering baggage tossed over the side, but revoked the command when furious passengers protested the maritime pollution. "Bits of clothing," noted a traveler, "could lodge themselves in the gullets of shark companions swimming alongside."

Throughout the tumult, Jonah dozed below deck, despite the tiny pillows customarily given long-distance travelers. His was an untroubled sleep, for he was sure an obstinate Lord had overstepped his authority.

The shipmistress figured that, in lieu of baggage, a person must be jettisoned, and she suggested casting lots. But Lot objected, stating, "Yes, it's true I should have blindfolded my Significant Other before she could turn into a pillar of salt, but that's no reason to make me the scapegoat." The discussion was interrupted when a steward pushed up a cart saying, "Your complimentary beverage and snack. . . . The choice of drink is wine or tainted water. And the food is spoiled hardtack."

After a leisurely repast, the shipmistress explained to Lot the intent was to cast lots, not a particular person. Her comment sparked a prolonged discussion of the trade-off between the revenues generated by legalized gambling versus the impact of betting on income-disadvantaged people who have less disposable income to risk.

During this free-wheeling debate the first mate—who was a ship officer, not the initial sex partner of a progressively minded spouse—panicked at the surging waves and called for abandoning ship.

"Myn and adults first!" he cried, avoiding a patronizing "Womyn and children first" slur that denies wompersons and preadults the honor of sacrificing themselves for the common cause.

But the shipmistress alertly countermynded the order, as the boat had discarded its Mae West life preservers due to objections over the jackets' sexist moniker. "Before consigning everyone to the drink," she directed, "let's give the lottery gambit a go."

So they drew straws in the downpour, and Jonah thought straws fitting given the amount of fresh drinking water suddenly available. With mounting tension, everyone took a straw, and each was the same size, until only one—Jonah's—was left. The jinxed traveler had drawn the most longitudinally disadvantaged piece of butchered plant matter!

Jonah then confided to all about Nineveh, and the Lord's imperious directive, and everyone empathized. "Who does the Lord think she is?" the shipmistress commented. "God?"

Meantime the waters roiled, and were tempestuous. When the mast snapped, the crew people took to the oars and rowed: No fuels from diesel engines fouled their pristine sea. Long-tailed rodent residents crept up from lodgings in steerage and abandoned ship. The crew rearranged the deck chairs. When that didn't work, they prayed, not to God necessarily, but to their respective gods, as the freethinking sail persons, in visits to distant shores like Delphi and Mount Olympus, had been exposed to varying conceptions of the Ultimate. But still it rained so much that, in comparison, Noah's ark seemed never to have left dry dock.

Out of desperation, the crew people knew they must make

a sacrificial lamb of Jonah, but as it was too wet to build a pyre they simply tossed him over the side. As he sailed toward the waves, Jonah cried, "Is it too late to purchase traveler's insurance . . .?"

He hit the water, and immediately *tempest fugit,* that is, the storm disappeared. Such abrupt shifts in the weather are symptomatic of global climate change.

The star-crossed traveler crashed below the surface and fell into the jaws of a posture-inhibited cetacean, whom some call the humpback whale. The sea dweller detested the taste of meat in her mouth but, sensing the vague bidding of a Higher Power, closed her eyes and gulped. Jonah tumbled down her vast gullet and would have broken his neck if not for the soft, blubbery skin lining the passageway.

He splashed to an undignified halt in a pool of saltwater within the cetacean's stomach. Soft light filtered down from a giant blowhole to illuminate a cavernous gut. The whale was large enough to have its own weather: Gentle updrafts flowed from the warmth of the creature's innards to the cooler air near the hole. A soaked Jonah heard the whale groan, and soon spotted the cause: The mast and rigging of *The Ill-Fated* was stuck in the creature's intestine! He gently pulled the debris from the intestinal tract, and the moaning ceased.

"Thank you," spake a voice from above, the words echoing off the arched walls of the immense belly. "I never know, when I go trawling for food, what I might pull in from you humans."

Grateful the cetacean companion had saved his life, Jonah offered to cleanse her sides of barnacles. "I'll climb up through the blowhole," he suggested, "and leave your exterior squeaky-clean." But the posture-inhibited whale would have none of it. "The barnacles and I enjoy a symbiotic relationship, Jonah. I provide them a mobile home, and in turn they attract plankton to my jaws. If I could, mind you, I'd eschew plankton and shrimp, and only chew greens like algae, but we whales are strapping, vigorous sorts who burn out without occasional high-protein meals."

And Leviathan grew fond of her codependent humyn companion and took him on a tour of the sea. "Come on up to my jaw, where you can enjoy the ocean view, and where we can speak without shouting." And lo, Jonah was like a surfer, gliding over soaring crests on the outstretched mouth of a graceful whale.

"The first thing you should know," lectured Leviathan, "is that the term for this body of water, Mediterranean, is a misnomer, and disturbingly jingoistic. This sea is not 'in the middle of all lands,' but is just a minor inlet of a far greater ocean. Any far-roaming fish will tell you that."

Impressed by his friend's knowledge, Jonah asked, "Are whales smarter than people?"

"Not smarter," the cetacean replied, "just wiser. We realize our place in Nature and are satisfied with it. None of this guff about gaining dominion over the earth."

"Is God a whale?" Jonah queried his friend.

"No," Leviathan modestly replied. "My own personal view—and I don't mean to impose my beliefs—is the earth herself is Goddess, and we are simply her manifestations."

Later, while gazing out on the waves, the twosome watched a fleet of massive olive-oil tankers lumber past. "This is one of my pet peeves, or domestic nonhumyn animal prisoner annoyances," the whale lamented. "When an olive-oil tanker sinks, a thick film covers the fins and feathers of fish and flying creatures happening by. In sipping for plankton, I've inadvertently swallowed liters of vegetable oil myself: It's nutritionally valueless, although it lowers my cholesterol dramatically. Given a fishy diet, sixteen hours of swimming a day, and regular doses of olive oil, I've got the circulatory system of a Greek Olympian."

A sailing ship cut through the tanker fleet and headed straight for Leviathan. The whale abruptly picked up speed, nearly throwing Jonah careening over the side, and just as abruptly dove, sending Jonah down her gullet again in a rushing cascade of sea water. The stunned traveler belly-flopped into the stomach pool and, spitting out brine, dragged himself onto a dry spot.

"What was that for?" Jonah shouted.

"I apologize, but it couldn't be helped," gasped his hostess from above. "The Israelites' King Ahab must have had a falling out with Jezebel again—whenever they have a spat, Ahab unwinds by going fishing, and he has this obsession about whales, especially melanin-impoverished ones. I've no desire to be turned into sashimi."

Jonah had barely struggled to his feet when the whale dove in a different direction, hurling him back into the brackish pool. When his head broke the surface, Jonah heard Leviathan's apologetic but angry voice resound off the stomach walls: "I'm sorry again for the lack of warning, but I was just visually harassed by a pack of sperm whales. I am a mammal, you know, and being a whale, rather well-endowed. The sperm whale is the most sexist species on the planet (with one exception), and I wasn't about to let my body be exploited!"

After things calmed down Jonah got to thinking, and he asked the whale to ferry him to Nineveh.

"Well," said Leviathan, "Sin City's not just on the other side of the pond. To get there we'd have to go clear around Africa."

And lo, centuries before Eurocentrics from Portugal accomplished the feat, a whale and a man from an underdeveloped region just kilometers from Africa were the first to circumnavigate that proud continent.

On reaching the coast of Babylon, Jonah, for nostalgia's sake, took one final douche in the bracing, briny waters of

Leviathan's gut. "I once was visually challenged," Jonah shouted up to her, "but now I see. I want to spread your way of thinking everywhere I go." Moments later the whale, blinking away a very salty, liter-sized tear, expelled Jonah by the usual method, and vomited him up on the shore.

Jonah made straightway for Nineveh, telling everyone along the way about his adventure. A few dismissed the tale as just another fish story, while most fled from Jonah coughing, given the ripeness of his clothes after his lengthy stay inside the whale's digestive tract. Jonah realized he'd been absent from society for quite some time when he saw his picture on milk cartons all over Babylon.

Upon reaching the city, Jonah preached to the ruler and the people about their errant ways. "Your town's landfill will run out of space by the next millennium," he ominously warned, "and since the Messiah is coming sooner than you imagine, the millennium is just around the corner."

The queen and her people repented, and turned their backs on conspicuous consumption. They put away their fancy apparel and put on sackcloth and ashes, taking pains to obtain the ashes from driftwood, not living plants, and certainly not tobacco. They placed sackcloth on their cattle companions as well, a nod to interspecies equality. For forty days and nights they fasted from animal carcass—and chic, pricey vegetarian restaurants cropped up like magic on every corner. The rate of victimless crime in Sin City fell, unintentionally, when nightly grayouts from a ban on whale-oil lamps led to greatly reduced business in the city's red light district.

And Jonah, his work in Babylon a success, trekked back to the sea and founded Greenpeace.

# he Three Self-Fulfilled Individuals

And in those days there went out a decree from Caesar Augustus that all the world should contribute to deficit reduction. And the decree was welcome, for the Romyn Empire, like most countries in most times, was undertaxed. The legitimate needs of the state, such as perpetual war and foreign occupations, and bread and circuses for longtime public assistance recipients, had to be met with revenue enhancements. The Rome Persons practiced real tax reform, and had done away with lengthy, complicated forms. Instead, they audited everyone, regardless of income. So Mary and Joseph, two carpenters living in Nazareth, gladly made arrangements for their yearly public-spirited donation. They went down to Bethlehem, a declining steel town filled with other blue-collar types. They were counted in the census, which more typically underreported fiscally disadvantaged persons like themselves.

That night an angel of the Lady appeared to several guards overseeing incarcerated sheep near a field of wheat. Announcing the imminent birth of a controversial but undeniably influential figure, the celestial envoy crafted a message with appeal both to monotheists and pagan worshippers of the winter solstice: "I bring you tidings of great joy concerning the Sun of god and the Light of the world." Then the angel flew away, leaving strange, circular crop markings on the wheat field.

At the same time, Joseph and his Significant Other, Mary—who was in the final stages of a common female work disability—could find no room at an inn. As it was a major holiday, reservations had filled up months before. They tried all the other inns but had trouble communicating with the foreign owners, all of whom hailed from the same East Indian immigrant family. Joseph grew anxious, for Mary could feel her pre-preadult kicking in her womb. She pointedly remarked, "Some regard such feistiness as the sure sign of a boy, as if womyn—far from being innately passive—aren't as innately aggressive as myn."

At length Joseph enticed the owners of an equestrian prison to grant their stable of inmates an evening of freedom, and while the horses frolicked outside, the Madonna gave birth in their manger. Upon delivery the newborn infant was gently slapped, and he promptly turned the other cheek. The Madonna should not be confused with *Madonna,* that icon of personal liberation, for *the* Madonna retained a quaint, obsolete habit of remaining loyal to a lone Significant Other.

THE POLITICALLY CORRECT GUIDE TO THE BIBLE 101

The preadult was named Jesus, pronounced "hay-ZOOS," and was given the honorific Emmynuel, pronounced "man-WELL." His last name, Christ, is often abbreviated "X," although this may offend admirers of another noted, latter-day prophet of color with an identical last name. Joseph, Jesus' father of step, proudly passed out smokeless cigars to Mary and, upon their return, the equestrian residents.

As she lay resting, Mary gazed outside at a tinseled, ornamented palm tree that constituted an insensitive and unnecessary display of religious symbolism in a semipublic place. She dreamily recalled the visitation nine months prior of the angel Gabrielle. The winged messenger had dropped in out of the blue to inform her she was with preadult, and would bring forth "a Sun of the Most Vertically Positioned." Although flattered, Mary noted the obvious fact she had no domestic incarceration partner.

"Devout people like you," Gabrielle scolded, "are too uptight about nontraditional families. With my connections, I can arrange for a Ms. to have a child all by her lonesome." The offer of childbearing without direct reliance on a man would have appealed to the latent feminist in any dame. "Think of yourself," the angel urged, "as the world's first surrogate mother." Overcome with emotion, Mary mumbled, "I am the handmaiden of the Lord," a lapse into a subservient class and gender role attributable to understandable shock over the stunning annunciation.

With the big news out of the way, Gabrielle gently chided the youthful Mary for her notorious celibacy, which lamentably lasted throughout her life. "These days, virginity puts a prewomyn at grave psychological and physical risk," it lectured. "Such a person will likely be ostracized, by friends and sex-ed teachers alike, for not conforming to peer-group expectations. She may even conclude that sex exists primarily for propagation, not personal gratification."

Mary thought this over and, seized with an odd sense of *déjà vu,* asked, "What did you say your name was?"

"You can call me Gabie."

"Didn't you visit my cousin-in-carceration Zechariah last year, and tell him he could also expect offspring?"

"You're correct—I'm getting quite the rep for bringing forth glad tidings of joy. Some folks, because of my wings I suppose, are mixing me up with the stork."

"I'm curious—is it hard being a member of the heavenly hostess?"

"Well, some have accused guardian angels like me, who are always looking over the shoulders of mortals, of violating their right to privacy, no matter how surreptitiously we do our jobs."

"I've always had a morbid fascination, Gabie—what was the war with Lucifer like?"

"Lucifer's violent minions had a decided edge in aggressiveness; our main advantage—we had God on our side. We also held the military high ground—Heaven. Some would argue, and I stress this is not meant to criticize Satan, that we also held the moral high ground. It was an exciting time to be alive, or even in Limbo. The Lord organized everyone into legions: The gentle strumming of harps was out, the martial blasts of trumpets were in. To be honest, I kind of miss Satan— he had his character flaws, but was basically misunderstood."

Mary's reverie ended with the unannounced entry into the equestrian holding pen of three camel companions, as well as their human sidekicks—the Three Self-Fulfilled Individuals.

"Hi," greeted the latter's leader, "we're three Gentiles from the East. I use the term East loosely, for it's a geographical convention imposed on this region by Western cartographers. I'm Caspar, the friendly *goy,* and these are my buds Melchior and Balthasar."

*Names like that and you're not Jewish?* wondered Mary.

"We come bearing gifts for your son of step—gold, francineincense, and myrrh. The stores were plumb out of swaddling clothes."

"Such extravagance was hardly necessary," said Joseph.

"We forgot," admitted Melchior, "about the stiff markup shops charge this time of year."

"And the lines!" cried Balthasar. "Thank goodness the bazaars were open late every night this week."

"If you'd like to buy more francineincense," Melchior told his hostesses, "you'd need only wait 'til the morrow. Most retailers post steep discounts on December twenty-sixth."

Joseph explained to the three non–Jewish Persons that the new holiday coincided with Hanukkah, in which a foreign king had tried to impose Greek culture on the Israelites.

"Given the tradition of scholarship among the Hebrews," remarked Balthasar, "I'd think they would have welcomed sororities and frats."

"No, not that kind of Greek culture," responded Joseph with some annoyance. "This king had the nerve to place a statue of Zeus in the main Jewish temple."

"Talk about striking a blow for cultural pluralism!" enthused Balthasar. "What became of this forward-looking ruler?"

"He was overthrown," said Joseph, "by devout rebels who were Hassidic."

Balthasar sympathized, "Couldn't they take anything for their indigestion?"

"Not acidic, *Hassidic!*" roared Joseph. "Anyway, Hanukkah's commemorated by lighting eight candles. Since Mary and I were raised Jewish, we hung candles on the palm tree. I kind of like the effect, don't you?"

"What," Mary asked the Three Self-Fulfilled Individuals, "do you guys do for a living?"

"We're court astrologers," replied Caspar. "I know it's

hard to believe, but some queens and First Womyn make decisions of state based on their daily horoscopes, or enhance their self-awareness by conversing with the deceased."

"Given such essential duties," remarked Joseph, "I'm amazed you could take time off for your journey."

"You know how it is," said Melchior. "So many people have vacation this week that it might as well be an official holiday."

"We're also court magicians," Caspar noted. "Through sleight of hand, smoke and mirrors, and cleverly staged events, we can make the charisma-challenged ruler seem sober, the most aged appear avuncular, the unethical flexible, the appeasing peace-loving, and the reckless dynamic. We're thinking of starting a public relations firm."

Mary poked at one of the gift wrappings. "What is myrrh anyway?"

"A terrific Scrabble term when you're hard up for a vowel," replied Caspar. "Myrrh, an aromatic plant, is also the most common holiday gift for a male, namely, 'old spice.'"

Melchior stated, "It's the ideal present for the deity who has everything."

Joseph interjected, "For three supposedly sharp fellows, you don't show much horse sense. I happen to know francineincense and myrrh are both strongly scented substances, and either could touch off a violent allergic reaction. Didn't you see the sign outside: 'This Stable Is a Fragrance-Free Zone'?"

"I wanted to complain about that posting," said Balthasar. "It's in Hebrew and Aramaic only, not Latin, and thus discriminates against the many recent Roman immigrants to these occupied territories, not to mention the ninety-five percent of the population who cannot read."

Melchior told Joseph, "We and three sweaty camels stop here after a thousand-kilometer trek through the blazing desert, and it's the smell of *incense* you complain about?"

"I'm serious," retorted Jesus' father of step. "If Bethlehem shuts down this detention center for a flagrant fragrance violation, my family is back in the street."*

"Well," asked Caspar, "what should we do with the toxic materials?"

"We could burn them as incense," suggested Balthasar.

Joseph held his tongue. "We're terribly short of space in here, so why don't you just stick them in the sweaty stockings I hung up over the fireplace?"

Upon leaving, the Three Self-Fulfilled Individuals ran into sheep guards seeking an elusive star of Bethlehem, and the astute astrologers, after making various astral calculations, were able to point to a blinding point of light directly over the stable. The sheep owners entered and, as they were all allergic to hay, loudly sneezed.

"'Bless you!" Mary and Joseph both cried, careful to omit that common phrase's initial reference to God, lest they presume the existence of a Higher Power with guests who may have been devoutly agnostic. The new arrivals brought with them additional gifts, and Joseph spent the next morning poring over toy assembly instructions.

Sadly, that hallowed, peaceful eve engendered a flood of baleful holiday customs. Harassment sprigs with the militaristic name of missiletoe were placed on ceilings to entrap unsuspecting feminists into unsolicited lip assignations. Whole forests were exterminated to make Christmas trees, topped all too often with angels or stars that inject a disturbing element of spirituality into an otherwise totally commercialized event.

Disturbing myths sprung up, such as the infamous legend of Santa Claus, an aged, tyrannical white male who expropri-

---

*A related statute to ban men's aftershave was rejected when someone noticed that every man of that period wore a beard.

ated a tract of prime North Pole real estate from its indigenous polar bear and Eskimo communities. The sinister Claus, who goes under various assumed identities, such as Kringle, Nicholas, and Von Bülow, founded a notorious sweatshop for extremely vertically challenged proletarians forced to labor around the clock for far-less-than-minimum-wage compensation (the elves work for free). The capitalist exploiter undercuts high-wage, high-quality, public-sector delivery services like the postal service with an all-women, slave-labor force of shackled reindeer companions that haul backbreaking loads at dizzying heights through almost unimaginable conditions of freezing wind and Arctic cold. In idle hours, Claus double-dips as a pliant shill for department store conglomerates seeking to addict impressionable preadults to conspicuous consumption.

The morning after Jesus' birth, Mary declared her firm intention to return to work the following day, but her sexist spouse insisted on a brief vacation in Egypt. Joseph himself needed a rest, having for months taken midnight shopping trips whenever Mary had uncontrollable cravings for kosher pickles and ice cream in a desert locale where frozen snacks were scarce. He may also have been influenced by reports that the local potentate, King Herod, was practicing strict demographic limitation on the region's newborn male progeny.

Upon crossing into Africa in late December, Mary, Joseph, and Jesus celebrated Kwanza. Like almost all people in Palestine and Egypt, the three were probably persons of color, so it was natural and fitting for them to take part in the Afrocentric Feast of the Winter Harvest. No doubt, after their central role in devising yet another sternly moralistic, monotheistic cult, they were anxious to lend active support to a purely nonreligious, nonheroic creed. Kwanza was a fitting epiphany to Christmas.

The Highly Esteemed Family returned from Africa on December 31 of the year 1 B.C.E. (Before the Current Era). As the travelers swayed through the Sinai on their derriere companions, gleeful shouts rung out from passing safari drivers:

"See you in the next millennium!"

"Don't forget to adjust your sundial to a different era entirely!"

In every oasis, notices were posted on palm trees advising everyone to switch to a D.C.E. (During the Current Era) convention the following day. For the umpteenth time, officials patiently explained the progression from one Year One to another Year One would proceed without an intervening annum because, as one procurator put it, "the Arabs haven't invented zero yet."*

Joseph told his spouse, "Let's hope the Romyns, after laboriously devising their newfangled Julian calendar, don't imperiously decide at the last minute to declare this a leap year, and add an extra day to December."

"Wouldn't that make it the *Thirteen* Days of Christmas?" replied Mary. "Not that I'm superstitious, but . . ."

". . . And an extra day of waiting," said Joseph, "would disappoint all the ardent partygoers who've spent months planning their once-in-a-thousand-years New Year's Eve bash."

---

*Some biblical scholars believe Jesus was born as late as 7 D.C.E., not 1 D.C.E. as previously thought. This means a future leap year will contain not one extra day, but six additional years.

# The Apostles, Jesus, and Diversity Awareness

Christ's itinerant life and restless search for meaning was rooted in his family background. As Jesus never knew his real dad, he was something of a latchkey child. His proletarian father of step was a wage slave in the hardscrabble carpentry trade. According to several accounts, Jesus had sisters and brothers, but he left them for a loose association of twelve unrelated men. His only long-term relationship, a platonic one, was with sex care provider Mary Magdalene.

The holidays were a time of special stress: Every other youth could expect two sets of gifts each year, but Jesus got only one, as his birthday fell on Christmas.

Jesus passed away three days prior to Earth Day, formerly called Easter, the former pagan festival of the spring. In some quarters, Easter is linked to a weird cult of the Bunny Rabbit, whose prolific procreation sets an atrocious example for an overpopulated planet. The holiday promotes the widespread boiling of poultry embryos and the poisoning of their protective shells with carcinogenic colored dyes. It fosters the mass consumption of jelly beans, which unlike true legumes are devoid of dietary fiber. Lastly, the festival's Easter bonnets and dresses push millions of innocent prewomyn into a premature path of fashion addiction.*

At the start of his public life, Jesus visited John the Baptist, who like many Baptists was a religious fundamentalist dwelling in a rural area. John immersed believers in the river Jordan, which in Hebrew means "dunk." He wore a leather girdle, perhaps to firm up an oversized tummy, although his diet of high-protein locusts and all-natural honey, and his constant presence in the water (swimming is the best exercise), should have kept him trim. Adhering to a priggish view of family values that owed more to Ozzie Nelson than Bob Packwood, John chided King Herod for wedding the Significant Other of his own male sibling, before Herod headed off the resulting controversy.

Upon arriving at the Jordan, Jesus observed that John's trade was prudently regulated. Anyone baptized had to wear a flotation device, and lifeguards were posted every ten meters along the shore of the shallow, barely moving rivulet. John strongly recommended nose clips and earplugs for his clients. For a nominal fee, longhaired prophets could rent bathing caps; they typically brought their own sandals.

---

*Because it has religious overtones, the term Easter can be replaced with Spring, as in "the White House's annual Spring Egg Roll."

As Jesus hesitated on the water's edge, John stated, "I know—it's you who should be baptizing me, Jesus—not the other way around."

"It's not that," replied the normally fearless evangelist. "The water's so *cold*."

"The best thing to do," counseled the experienced bather, "is to jump right in. In a minute or two you'll get used to it, though your toes might tingle a bit. And you have to duck your halo. Just getting the feet wet won't cut it."

John gently but firmly pushed the reluctant wader under the surface. When Jesus emerged, he asked, "Do you have any swaddling clothes?"

"You mean for a bathing suit?"

"No, it's just that I feel born again."

Soon after he started preaching, Jesus stopped a crowd from stoning a woman to death by declaring, "Let he who is ethically unchallenged cast the first stone." Indeed, stone violence was the bane of Judea, so authorities strictly regulated the sale and possession of rocks. By law, stones could be picked off the ground only after a forty-day-and-forty-night waiting period. An "assault boulders" ban was instituted, with an exception for military uses like catapults. Sharpening of rocks was permitted, up to a point. Laws on the books against tossing pebbles were seldom enforced.

To help track down those breaking the stone-control laws, officials tried etching a serial number in every rock, but the personpower demanded for the immense task proved daunting. Authorities attempted a buyback of all stones in circulation, but this only drained the treasury without causing a noticeable reduction in the number of weapons strewn about Palestine's rocky soil. So a stiff tax was placed on quarries. Stonecutters and masons were sued for fashioning the instruments of violence.

Stone enthusiasts contended these actions denied citizens the means to defend themselves from despots. "When the government has a monopoly on slingshots and other spheroid-hurling devices," argued a lobbyist for the Nazareth Rock Association, "average folk have no tools to thwart tyranny." Rock proponents pushed for a "hidden stone law" in which a person traveling through a dangerous neighborhood could hide a stone ax under her cloak for self-defense.*

Meanwhile, Jesus, moralistic as always, insisted on condemning violence of any sort, claiming: "The fault lies not so much in our stones, but in ourselves."

One day, Jesus came upon Simon and Andrew, two fisherpersons plundering the Sea of Galilee. (The "sea" of Galilee is really a lake; no slight is intended the noble body of water.) The terrible twosome, fortunately, hadn't strangled a fish all day, and Jesus, speaking metaphorically, suggested they cast their net in deeper waters. They did, literally speaking, but fortunately their net, filled to the breaking point, burst. They cast another net, and another boat came over to help, and both of the murderous vessels, fortunately, floundered from the weight of the catch.

As a humbled Simon and Andrew sat soaked on the shore, Jesus chastised them: "How would you feel if you reached for fruit on a tree, and a hook seized your hand, and you were yanked into the air and couldn't breathe? How does that differ from your treatment of fish?"

"We realize our work is insensitive, Lord," said Andrew. "Fish have complex neural networks and experience pain just like people do."

"Maybe," said Simon, "we should dispense with nets, which indiscriminately vanquish edible fish as well as unintended victims, and go back to fishing rods, which only slaughter one at a time."

---

*Many present-day protestors in the West Bank still actively espouse the right to bear stones.

"Or ban our assassinations altogether with a Sea of Galilee catch-and-release program," said Andrew.

But Jesus pointed out that hooked fish, even when released, suffer from severe lactic acid buildup.

"And fish," agreed Andrew, "are awfully hard to burp."

Simon added, "We're not even discussing the bait worms and flies that are drowned or eaten alive."

"Or," added Andy, "the negative implications for fisher-persons of fish slaughter: seasickness, sunburn, beer hangovers."

"Come," Jesus responded, "and I will make of you fishers of myn. Metaphorically speaking, of course."

Simon and Andrew threw down their asphyxiation devices and followed him, without giving their supervisor two weeks' notice.

Jesus selected ten other close advisors, and upon becoming Christians, a remarkable change was wrought on the swarthy, Mediterranean Semites: Their eyes seemed bluer, their skin pinker, hair less frizzy, noses more peaked, accents more sub-urban. Conversation at the dinner table grew less contentious but also blander. To the surprise of Jewish friends, the apostles began smearing mayonnaise on their matzoh. Even their names—Pete, Andy, Phil, and Tom—seemed less ethnic.

The disciples were added after the *Jerusalem Herald* ran a classified ad:

---

# WANTED

Rapidly growing startup firm seeks to expand customer base throughout the Mediterranean. Communication specialists needed to preach contro-versial doctrine to sometimes hostile audiences. Must be willing to put up with banishment, torture, or untimely ends by lion feeding. Experience in miracle-

working not required; will train. Fluency in Aramaic
and Hebrew essential; knowledge of Greek and Latin
a plus, although speaking in tongues may supersede
this qualification. Salary nominal, but benefits include
an unsurpassed retirement package in a veritable
paradise. Equal opportunity employer: This is an ecu-
menical, universalist faith.

After job interviews, Jesus and his band would discuss the
applicants, with the disciples generally eager to hire but the
more critical Jesus asking, "I know he can do the work, but
can he walk on water?" One outstanding performer was the
apostle John, a marketing whiz who'd wheedle stadium front-
row seats for every gladiatorial bout and hold a placard read-
ing "John 3:16" to hype his own newsletter.

Despite impressive occupational skills, the apostles lacked
diversity. According to certain traditions, they were all male
and Christian. No attempt was made to recruit Pharisees or
Sadducees. However, Afrocentric scholars believe all were
black, while authoritative Euroeccentrics like Randy Weaver
and the Montana Militia are convinced each was of Aryan
descent. (To verify these assertions, DNA tests should be performed on the Shroud of Turin.) Other experts, noting the
beards, flowing robes, and otherworldly pronouncements of
the group, believe they hailed from Taos, New Mexico.

In spreading the gospel, the impoverished disciples usually
stayed with friends or camped on the roadside, for the fledg-
ling Young Men's Christian Association had established discount hostels in just a few towns. But one cold evening the
apostles rented a budget inn. As they warmed themselves at the
fireplace, Jesus appointed his successor, stating, "Upon this
rock, Peter, I build my church"—and the smoke leaving the
chimney turned from black to white.

Peter soon put on vicarious airs. He annoyed the other

apostles by uttering phrases of Caesar's hated occupiers—*pax vobiscum, in nomine patris, quo vadis.* In fact, he was seized with a passion to visit Rome, and to collect priceless objects of Greco-Roman art. When Mary Magdalene answered a want ad for an apostolic position, Peter insisted on a male-only club. He traveled while standing in an odd protective carriage covered with a rectangular box of transparent, spear-proof material. Peter later became a harshly judgmental doorkeeper of heaven denying entry to those deemed morally disadvantaged.

He was nearly forced to resign from his earthly duties after his impromptu infamous remark that "womyn are the weaker vessel." His slip of the tongue ignited a firestorm of criticism from womyn's lefts groups. "Femails have greater intelligence, healthier diets, and more endurance," inveighed the head of the Nazareth Organization for Wompersuns. "And this single white male has the nerve to claim superiority?"

The first pope compounded his error by pontificating: "I was misinterpreted—I meant to say 'the weaker sex.'" But the apostle Judas betrayed his defense by stating, "I don't see Peter raising kids and working a full-time job at the same time." Peter only salvaged his job by shaving his head, donning sackcloth and ashes, and, while brandishing a cat-o'-nine-tails for self-flagellation, shouting "*Mea culpa!*" before an irate assemblage of gender activists and sympathetic media scribes. As penance for his unconscionable offense, Peter recited ten thousand Our Parents.

# esus and His Miraculous Malpractices

*Among the archeological finds in the Biologically Challenged Sea Scrolls was a news story about the unintended consequences of Jesus' special powers.*

**Jerusalem, Palestine. April 1, 30 D.C.E.** An incensed local magistrate today suspended the preaching license of evangelist Jesus Christ for conducting legally suspect miracles. Since starting his ministry three years ago, Christ has cured scores of the optically hindranced, hearing-impaired, mentally different, motionally restricted, differentially healthy, verbally hindered, and other handi-capable individuals, even raising the biologically challenged from a state of terminal inconvenience.

A major focus of the preliminary hearing was Christ's unauthorized raising of his friend Lazarus. That resurrection, corroborated by several witnesses and the startling testimony of Lazarus himself, provoked a flurry of threatened legal action against Christ and the family of the formerly deceased.

In a jammed courtroom, the irate undertaker for the inter-rupted burial discussed a bitter financial row between herself and Martha, the sibling of Lazarus.

"Martha has the gall to demand a refund for the purchase of the tomb. Purchase? It was a short-term rental! I'm entitled to that money, and maybe damages as well, because no one will use that grave site again—they think it's haunted. Meantime my clientele has shrunk to nothing; people are scared to death I'll bury them alive."

The coroner for Lazarus testified that the unexpected rais-ing had ruined his professional reputation. "From now on," he groaned, "death certificates bearing my signature won't be worth the parchment they're written on." The coroner, dis-missed by the city morgue for incompetence, broke down on the witness chair before vowing to sue Jesus for lost wages.

A friend of the resurrected filed a class-action suit against Jesus. "When the neighborhood kids saw Lazarus walk out of that tomb like an Egyptian mummy, his funeral wrappings trailing on the ground, they were traumatized for life. Who knows how long they'll need therapy?" A second suit by cured persons asserts Christ's miracles undercut prior legal motions to collect pain-and-suffering damages. These plaintiffs have refused to turn in disabled-person parking stickers for their carriages.

Estate lawyers for Lazarus and an uncle who had inherited half his property clashed over the Comeback Kid's will. "To pay off debtors, I sold the property as soon as I got it," the uncle stated in a deposition. "I can't be held liable for getting it back."

Another monetary tiff entails the life insurance paid Martha upon the passing of Lazarus. "Her attitude is, 'Sorry, no refunds,' but we must differ," said the insurance firm's attorney. "The surviving party is by definition *not* a widow after the unconventional return of a deceased spouse.

"If the court lets Martha retain these funds, it will establish a far-reaching precedent that gives others a strong incentive to pass away—in the expectation they'd enjoy a hefty payment on returning from the afterlife. Your Honor, there is enormous potential for kickbacks from soon-to-be-deceased persons to resurrecting preachers less scrupulous than the unconventional but highly ethical Mr. Christ."

Another attorney, with the Aramaic Medical Association, made a powerful case for barring Christ from practicing medicine. "First, he hasn't a medical degree. In fact, he lacks formal education of any kind. No medical college will recognize his uncertified home-schooling degree in comparative religions.

"Second, he violates standard medical practice by declining to ask about preexisting medical conditions before treating a patient. Nor does he first conduct a battery of expensive tests to spike the doctor's bill and protect himself against bogus malpractice suits. In many of his treatments, by the way, he flouts well-established procedures that call for bleeding the infirm instead of effecting a complete and instantaneous recovery.

"Third, he doesn't charge for his expertise, even though the going rate for a doctor's visit is 800 denarii. Further, in working for free, Christ violates ministers' union rules on payment of the prevailing wage to miracle workers."

An official with the Roman Food and Drug Agency acknowledged Christ's robe had remarkable healing powers.

"Some patients are relieved of life-threatening ailments just by touching it," the parchment pusher noted. "However, any medical device, drug, or technique must go through a mandatory process of regulatory review, and extensive rounds of laboratory testing, before being allowed on the market. The cesarean section first performed for Rome's greatest general over one hundred years ago is only now being approved for general use. I would strongly advise Jesus to wear a tunic or toga until his robe receives official sanction."

After a luncheon recess, spectators were riveted by Lazarus' testimony about his temporary absence. "After I passed on," he stated, "I had the eerie sensation of floating over a sickbed. Looking down, I could see myself stretched out on the sheets. But I no longer felt any connection with my physical body. Moments later, I found myself traveling through a long, dark tunnel. This journey continued at great speed for an indeterminate time. A pinpoint of light became perceptible at the end of the tunnel, and it grew into a circle of glowing light. When I reached the tunnel's terminus, I saw a luminous figure who looked remarkably like my friend Jesus. The next thing I knew, the rock from my tomb had been rolled away, and there stood Christ himself."

Following the recess, the hearing probed other complaints relating to Christ's special powers. A sorrowful farmer recalled, "I'd endured a months-long drought when a mighty tempest wracked the land; the life-giving rain had finally come. But it mysteriously stopped as soon as it started." He later learned that Jesus, while walking on the surface of the nearby lake, had calmed the storm, which threatened to swamp his ship-borne disciples. "It hasn't rained since; I had to plow under my crops," grieved the farmer. "I demand compensation!"

Both plaintiffs and the bench berated the accused for performing unsolicited exorcisms. A breeder of porcine companions described how Christ had expelled free-spirited sprites vilified as "evil spirits" out of a cerebrally challenged individual and into the bodies of his piglets.

"Driven by the visiting sprites, or perhaps seized with panic, the unfortunate animals stampeded into a pond and drowned. Now I know folks agree to disagree on whether or not it's kosher to eat porcine companions, or any other nonhuman animals, and I concede that eating them contributes to clogged arterial walls and higher blood pressure. But this minister fellow has no business messing with the minds of my pigs."

Presiding judge Pontius Pilate informed Christ that his "exorcisms are impressive feats likely to turn the heads of interested observers. Yet this court is fed up with the way you evangelists marginalize these supposedly ethically suspect souls. You evict them from their temporary homes without due process, forcing them to hastily relocate to the next available host. If you insist on continuing this procedure, I order you to provide them with advice on and financial assistance for securing a new abode."

The magistrate chided Christ for disdaining long-ignored disabilities now widely recognized as requiring expert care. "You should expand your considerable healing powers into such critical fields as gambling addiction, swearing dependency, sex addiction, attention deficit disorders like short attention spans, and uncontrollable impulse affliction leading to habitual overeating."

Later, a merchant documented the disruptive effect of another well-known miracle on the local economy: "When Jesus fed five thousand famished pilgrims with two measly fish and five chunks of bread, the price of seafood and pastries fell through the floor. He left at least a dozen baskets of leftovers, and this unused inventory put further downward pressure on prices. Half the bakers in my village are on workfare, and the seafood shops still can't charge enough to turn a profit."

The disciple known as Doubting Thomas testified he'd

been dubious of the food giveaway: "I told Jesus we should charge something at these public gatherings—you make all your money on concessions." In contrast, the financially savvy apostle Matthew, a former tax-collecting publican, recalled his excitement: "I urged Jesus to franchise the idea. Think of it: a string of Arthur Preacher's seafood restaurants throughout Galilee!"

Pontius Pilate ruled that the apostles broke food safety regulations by not donning disposable gloves before distributing the victuals. He rebuked Mr. Christ for lacking even the required vendor's license or park permit for feeding the five thousand.

Nor did the evangelist, according to a lawyer with the Cana town council, obtain a vintner's license before transforming jars of water into wine at a raucous wedding celebration. "Well into the night," chided the attorney, "constables fielded neighbors' complaints about the loud noise of the festivities. But more damning from a public health standpoint was Christ's failure to place on the containers clearly marked warning labels about the risks of wine consumption."

Silent through most of the proceedings, the normally forgiving Jesus was then stricken by compassion fatigue. He cried at his tormentors, "Woe unto you, lawyers! For ye lay on men's shoulders burdens grievous to be borne," before being gaveled silent and threatened with contempt of court.

The lawyer nervously took up her testimony. "To be fair, a warning label should note that a daily cup of wine taken with dinner may actually lower the risk of heart disease. It's also my understanding, based on favorable comments by the wedding's host—who mistakenly believed the best wine had been served first, instead of saved until the guests were inebriated—that Jesus' spontaneous concoction had the taste and bouquet of vintage wine. Still, his callous neglect of the public's health raises serious concerns.

"Judge, you wouldn't believe my frustration in trying to cut consumption of alcohol in a Mediterranean, Judeo-Jesusian culture where wine is not only celebrated as the table drink of choice, but revered as a sacrament in religious ceremonies."

The suspension of Christ's preacher's license will last forty days, during which time Jesus Christ is expected to maintain a low public profile by practicing transcendental meditation in the desert. He pledged, at any future weddings, to turn any unlabeled alcoholic substance into water. To pay off the costly claims against him, Pilate urged Christ to supplement his meager preacher's income with a better compensated position, such as money changing in a temple.

# Politically Corrected Proverbs

*This chapter contains proverbs\* and parts of psalms and parables from both the Chronologically Gifted Testament and the Somewhat Less Seasoned Ovament.*

Ye are the light, and the dark, of the world—and the gray. A city on a hill, or in a valley or on a plain, cannot be hid.

Wine maketh glad the heart of man, and should not be drunk during pregnancy, and impairs the ability to operate machinery, and may cause health problems.

The harvest truly is plenteous, but the laborers are few, for they've been downsized.

---

\*The term "proverb" does not imply preference or special treatment for a verb. This book neither favors nor discourages the use of verbs, pronouns, adverbs, adjectives, nouns, prepositions, punctuation marks, or any other particle or part of speech.

If thou choose to get theeself hence, Satan, thou mayest.

Thou art weighed in the balances, and art found wanting. Thou art a fatism survivor.

Woe unto them that call ethically challenged ethically enhanced, and ethically enhanced ethically challenged.

A den of unconventional income transfer specialists.

Government is our refuge and our strength. Therefore fear we not though the earth be moved and mountains carried into the sea, for the Federal Emergency Management Agency shall provide disaster relief.

Every man and woman child among you shall be circumcised.

There is nothing covered that shall not be revealed, nor hid that shall not be known, for the Special Prosecutor has power of subpoena and unlimited funds.

Man does not live by granola alone.

Yea, though I walk through the valley of the shadow of death, I shall fear no evil, for "evil" and "good" are mere logical constructs.

When I was a preadult, I spake as a preadult, I understood as a preadult, I thought as a preadult: But when I became an adult, I put away the things of a preadult.

Out of the mouths of sex objects.

What therefore God hath joined, let all put asunder through no-fault divorce.

Be no more tossed to and fro, and carried about with every wind of doctrine—the election is over.

Whosoever putteth away his wife, and marrieth another, committeth not adultery, but taketh a trophy wife.

Withhold correction from the child, for if thou slappest him he'll sue.

I now pronounce you domestic partners. You may now kiss the spouse.

Whosoever diggeth a pit shall fall within, and apply for workman's comp.

O ye of vertically disadvantaged faith.

Money is the root of all behavioral divergence.

Do not turn to mediums or wizards, other than to converse with Eleanor Roosevelt.

And they began to speak in tongues, and every man heard them in his own language, because of bilingual education programs.

No man can serve two mistresses.

Eat no-fat foods; drink non-alcoholic beverages; and try to be merry.

I was directionally challenged, but now am found.

There was a certain fiscally advantaged persun, and a certain alms solicitor named Lazarus, and the former suffered from compassion fatigue.

It is more blessed to give than to receive, especially through a tax-deductible charity organization.

The visually inhibited leading the visually inhibited.

Upon Peter, this rock, I will build my faith community.

If any provide not for his own, and specially not for those of his own house, he be an elective father.*

Our Parent, who art in heaven.

O sing unto the Lord a new song, but parents be advised: explicit lyrics.

The alleged human rights violations of the innocents.

They done got mouths, but they don't speak nothing; eyes they got, but they don't see nothing; they done got ears, too, but they don't hear nothing no how. (Ebonics version)

The way of the leisure-oriented (slothful) man is as a hedge of thorns.

The race is not to the quickness-endowed.

Self-esteem of self-esteems, all is self-esteem.

In the name of the Parent, and the Youth, and the Spiritually Enhanced Out-of-Body Experiencer. Amen.

---

*Deadbeat dad.